The Film Experience

THE
FILM
EXPERIENCE

Elements of Motion Picture Art

BY

ROY HUSS

AND

NORMAN SILVERSTEIN

A DELTA BOOK

A DELTA BOOK

Published by
DELL PUBLISHING CO., INC.
750 Third Avenue,
New York, N. Y. 10017

Reprinted by arrangement with
Harper & Row, Publishers, Incorporated, New York
Manufactured in the United States of America
Third Printing

Contents

Illustrations

ix

Acknowledgments

We wish to express our gratitude to the following institutions and individuals.

For permission to reproduce stills and other illustrative materials we thank American International Pictures, Audio Film Center, Columbia Pictures Corp., Contemporary Films, Inc., Embassy Pictures Corp. and Joseph E. Levine, Janus Films, Inc., Paul Killiam, Pare Lorentz Associates, Inc., United Artists Associated, and Universal Pictures. We are particularly grateful to Repix, Inc., for permission to reproduce parts of the storyboard of *The Sands of Iwo Jima*; to Van Praag Productions, Inc., of New York for permission to reproduce the wipe chart from *Color It Van Praag*; to the Film School of Lodz, Poland, for supplying a shot analysis of *Citizen Kane*; to the Central Film Archives at Warsaw for production stills from Wajda's *Samson*; and to the Museum of Modern Art in New York for supplying prints of numerous stills.

For permission to quote part of Eisenstein's script for *Ferghana Canal* we wish to thank Harcourt, Brace & World, Inc.; for the poem "Epigram" by J. V. Cunningham, the estate of Alan Swallow; for six lines of verse from *The River*, Pare Lorentz Associates, Inc. For their kindness in letting us quote from our own articles we thank the editors of *College English* and the board of the National Council of Teachers of English, the editor of *Japan Quarterly*, and the editor of *Salmagundi: A Quarterly of the Humanities & Social Sciences*.

Among the many individuals who have been both helpful and encouraging are Robert Ball of Queens College, who supplied valuable advice on research and publication procedures, and James D. Allen of New York, who read and criticized the manuscript.

Thanks are due Barbara Pritchard and Jan Howells of Columbia Pictures, and Milton and David Moshlak of Filmways, Inc., for making it possible for us to witness the various phases of film production. In Poland, special acknowledgments must go to Jerzy Toeplitz, rector of the Polish State Film School at Lodz, and to others who, with Mr. Toeplitz's permission, made workshops, studios, and libraries throughout Poland available for study: Messrs. Jacek Mieroslawski, Stanislaw Olegniczak, Barry Clayton, and members of the Instityt Sztuki, Central Film Archives, and Film Polski in Warsaw. Mr. Gérard Conio deserves special thanks for introducing us to many film artists.

Above all, we owe an incalculable debt to Norbert Slepyan, our editor at Harper & Row, who encouraged our ideas from their very inception, and carefully and patiently nurtured them to fruition in this book.

The Film Experience

CHAPTER ONE

The Film Experience

Since moviegoers do not have to be told what a movie is, critics seem presumptuous when they write about cinema as art. When they lay stress on cinematic details and employ technical terms, finding analogies between film and painting or literature, moviegoers find critics pretentious as well. The film is so clearly a part of one's growing up that one naturally looks down on those who make movies an experience comparable to listening to Beethoven, looking at Picasso, or reading Milton. The film is a Saturday afternoon entertainment during which James Cagney shoves grapefruit into Mae Clarke's "kisser," Godzilla flies, Steve Reeves as Hercules breaks his chains, and Rory Calhoun gets out of a tight spot. On TV, movies are bedtime stories for adults in which problems, hard in life to get into and impossible in life to solve, absorb the interest of those who like hard problems and easy solutions. Why the fuss about cinema as art?

Even when classicists, historians, philosophers, professors of fine arts, and other intellectuals—people who ought to know better—praise films, their tributes are for the film "subculture." To them, the most appealing feature of the movies is naïveté and spontaneity, which they fear will come to harm if films are subjected to the discipline of other arts and sciences. In their view, the moviegoer should not spoil his fun by applying aesthetic judgment. Rather he should let himself go, and seek total immersion.

Yet there is another notion of film "culture," which has been growing stronger of late. Although the majority of people think of cinema as mere entertainment—"escapism"—the fact that film has always been a legitimate art form has not gone unnoticed, or even unpublicized. *Time*

1

magazine, for example, has spoken of the necessity for the modern intellectual to become "cineliterate." Elia Kazan has announced on television that for intellectual and artistic stimulation, *he* goes not to the theater but to the movies. Even the earliest uses of moving pictures were not to entertain, but to put reality in a new light for the sake of better perceiving it. As early as 1871, theoreticians were concerned with discovering through cinematography the operation of things invisible to the human eye. Through their work, how a bird flies and a horse gallops became "magically" clear. They did not themselves regard what they were doing as art, for it was all in the name of scientific research; but it was a short time after those earliest endeavors that film pioneers recognized the art potential in film making. By 1915 such a formidable poet as Vachel Lindsay could see in movies a way of bringing to life that which is necessarily static in painting and sculpture. During the twenties and thirties, Sergei Eisenstein was developing a *poetics* of the film, pointing out that not only does film delight and teach, as do the other arts, but that it also has its own particular "form" and "sense."

How potent film expression can be was soon recognized by those who could use it and by those who feared it. Lenin and Hitler relied enormously on films to carry the propaganda of Bolshevism and Nazism to their own people and around the world. In so doing, they inadvertently advanced film art. Eisenstein's genius found its first impetus under Lenin's commissions. Leni Riefenstahl's *Olympia,* covering the 1936 Olympic Games, advertised "the superiority of the German race" and the principle of "strength through joy" in a poetic documentary. John Grierson's *Night Mail* (1936),* conceived to demonstrate the excellence of the British Postal Service, became a visual celebration of transportation with the help of a text by W. H. Auden.

When moving pictures were first shown to the public, they were an immediate success, which is not surprising, for they appealed directly to a fundamental human thirst—a thirst for the exhibition and imitation of people and things. No doubt a part of the movies' early popularity was the novelty of the thing, this great, flickering toy. But rather than waning, the appeal of the "toy" became world-wide. Those first films of the nineties—films of trains pulling into stations or of sea waves crashing on rocks, and the first "shocker," Edison's *The Kiss* (1896)—astounded the audiences of the nickelodeons by their power to capture and repro-

* Dates are based on public premières, except when the official opening was long delayed because of censorship, or, as for underground films, because of the lack of commercial distribution. In such cases the date of completion, when known, is given.

duce over and over again a moment of stark reality. Those people had themselves seen trains pulling into stations, waves crashing against rocks, and people actually kissing, but somehow the moving pictures made these things different and more exciting, mysteriously so, especially when one considers how much of the "actual" events was not shown. There was no color, the activity was silent, and even the movement was jerky and unnatural. The film was spotted and grainy, and in place of that ever-searching quality of the human eye, the camera eye was but a framed, fixed stare. To all intents and purposes, these audiences should have had a better time going to train stations themselves to watch the trains come in—and that wouldn't have cost a nickel. Yet excitement over the enlarging horizons of photographic realism was universal. In France, for example, the Lumière brothers in the 1900's set up their cameras to capture the passing scene on the streets of Paris, while in America the Edison Company was sending cameramen out to film Niagara Falls. What held the early film audiences and brought them back for more was the delight of seeing reality reproduced and at the same time transformed—the familiar made strange.

A refinement of this kind of pleasure has been the public's fascination with "true-to-life" re-enactments. The movies suddenly made it possible to see people and events of note for oneself, as they actually lived or happened. Thus the growth of the newsreel. As early as 1898 the first of the new breed of newsreel war cameramen were in Cuba shooting Teddy Roosevelt and his Rough Riders, making TR one of the first of a line of politicians whose images have been caught and enhanced by films.

From shots of simple happenings and from those early—sometimes staged—newsreels developed the true art form of the documentary. Under John Grierson, Pare Lorentz, and Robert Flaherty, the filming of the real took on the impact of brilliant drama. In their hands, the familiar and unfamiliar elements of life itself became the raw materials of artistic (and political, social, and economic) statements. Since then, Louis de Rochemont and other directors have used documentary techniques in fiction films, and a brilliant new concept of the documentary has developed in the style of *cinema vérité*.

Since most of the film footage produced these days is for commercial, educational, and scientific use, "research films" in their purest form are very much with us. Moreover, they are greatly similar in purpose to the very first moving pictures. Instead of the mechanics of flight, the subject may be the workings of a missile or space capsule. Rather than shoot the galloping of a horse, such film makers may shoot through an electron microscope to record the functions of the tiniest organisms. At their best they fulfill Siegfried Kracauer's ideal of using film to "redeem physical reality."

Even in frankly fictionalized movie stories the viewer expects authenticity, and so film makers must keep on hand whole libraries of "stock" footage of places, processes, and events, shots which are quite similar to those early nickelodeon renderings of the real world on film. Thus films about newspapers can show rolling presses; stories involving travel can draw upon shots of ships, airplanes, famous cities, or quaint out-of-the-way places. The soaring airplane that often breaks into a human drama is likely to come from the studio library, as is the moving traffic seen through the back window in a taxi scene. Such footage can be projected by back projection to serve as a background for the actors in the studio. Other library stock shots may be used for authenticity, as in the use of newsreel combat film in war stories. In such ways as these do seemingly unmalleable materials such as locales, processes, or simple actions become workable into larger artistic wholes.

To achieve particular effects and integrate them into the total film, the film editor groups, cuts, conjoins, and superimposes various research shots; in short, handles them as if they were plastic material. A film maker does not simply present raw reality; he uses what he has photographed to make a point. Newsreel footage, for example, can be cut up and even mixed with still photographs so that the intercutting causes a point of view to emerge. Bruce Conner accomplished just that in *Report* (1965) by juxtaposing newsreel footage of the house in which Lincoln died with shots of the Kennedy motorcade moving through Dallas toward the book depository. By joining these two research elements, Conner created a kind of simile and established a theme. Documentarists always engage in such manipulation, but Conner here creates a new kind of documentary by means of rapid cutting and cross-cutting, nonsynchronous sound, disrupted time order, repeated segments of action, and reversed motion. The assassination of President Kennedy is, to be sure, "reported," through authentic footage of the motorcade and a tape of the radio coverage of those confused events. However, Conner entirely reshapes this material to bring out its essence. Violent cutting emphasizes the violence of the homicide itself; repeating the sight of the President in the automobile just before the shooting drives home its dreadful inevitability; and reversing the motion of the car as it is seen from the rear, so that it appears several times to back into the camera, panders to our futile desire to pull the President back from his fate. By intercutting these specially handled scenes with such shots as those of Lincoln's house and of President Kennedy's wedding, Conner seems to add irrelevant documentary data, but actually adds meaning and poignancy. After all, is not historiography itself the reordering of facts into a meaningful context or pattern?

A "pure" rendering of objective reality is actually impossible. Shaping always occurs. The Lumières' shots of Paris seem to be raw, untampered-with material. But even here the cameraman has selected the placement of his camera, has adjusted the light values and distorted or changed the focal length. Imaginative shaping of various kinds has always been part and parcel of film making. Early film artists were quick to find ways of arranging scenes and to invent photographic trickery that could compete with—and even surpass—those found in "live" vaudeville and magic shows. In France, Georges Méliès, and in America, Edwin Porter, presented "spectacle films," dazzling in their ingenuity, toward which the audience was expected to maintain a "willing suspension of disbelief." It *Coleridge* was quite within the range of their ambition to make films with inanimate objects as actors (the seemingly self-propelled furniture in *The Automatic Moving Company*, France, 1910) and even to show "a trip to the moon"—a subject perennially challenging to moviemakers. If we can visualize Méliès hauling a huge papier-mâché moon up a ramp toward the camera as he made his *A Trip to the Moon* in 1902, we can get an idea of the fervor and imagination with which creators of film spectacles go about their work.

While the research film presumes to present undistorted reality, the spectacle purports to invent reality. Yet just as the research film cannot present unaltered truth, so the spectacle usually involves research elements: objects, events, or locales which the audience delights in seeing because they can be verified as "real." It is reported that when Erich von Stroheim made *Foolish Wives* (1922),

he had installed a complete electrical wiring system for each room of a dummy hotel that appeared briefly in the film. In another picture he ordered $10,000 worth of special medals to be struck off for officers in the army of a mythical kingdom, had the royal crest embroidered on his players' underclothes, held up a costly scene for hours until the smoke from a single chimney was rising to his satisfaction. Such details, he argued, may not have added to the physical reality of his pictures, but they did enhance the feeling, the atmosphere that he was trying to create.[1]

Publicity men know the value of these research units in making a film attractive. They know that people want to see "real" things. De Mille used to boast that his movie decor was real or was copied precisely from the baths of Caracalla; and James Agee noted that "in *Wilson* they copied the cracks on the paintings in the White House."[2] Hollywood especially has always been capable of exploiting a paradox which, as we have seen, movie audiences always relish: fascination with a perfect illusion of reality, and an added titillation in knowing that what they are seeing is, after all, only an illusion created for the sake of spectacle.

Film makers intrigue moviegoers not only with the starkness or richness of visual details of experience, but also by the "real" scenes they can evoke without actually photographing them. A noise of splashing water while the camera focuses on two characters sitting on a rock can evoke the image of a nearby waterfall. Or the actual photographing of one object or locale can suggest the presence of another, if the director "composes" his frame with the same care exercised by a painter. By arranging lines, colors, and planes, a painter may draw the eye to an object in the foreground or send it scampering along a winding road into the misty horizon of the background, thus suggesting a world beyond the viewer's ken and expanding the confines of the canvas. The film maker has a similar means by which he can evoke a much larger scene than he actually shows. When, in *Ashes* (1965), Wajda allows the black smoke from burning houses to burst beyond the confines of the frame, his already grandiose tableau (reminiscent of Antigone burying her dead brother) is expanded even further (Fig. 1). This kind of movement is most effective when the total composition avoids a sense of centrality, that is, when no key figure or object is placed in the center of the frame. In Roberto Rossellini's *The Little Flowers of Saint Francis* (1950), the dispersing of the monks in all directions in the film's last sequence implies the existence beyond the range of the camera of a Catholic world which the monks will spiritually reunify by their preaching.

Besides the never-to-be-seen reality that is provided by having objects move off-camera, or off-frame, film makers can induce a sense of an about-to-be-discovered reality. For this purpose they move the camera left or right (the pan shot) or up and down (the tilt shot) or place it on tracks to follow and catch up with a moving actor or object. By panning slowly, the camera makes things gradually swim into the moviegoer's field of vision. In a mystery or suspense story, the camera panning over a semidarkened room and alighting on unexpected objects stimulates fearful conjectures about the next object it will discover. A subtler method of implying, rather than photographing, realistic details involves editing filmstrips. A famous example occurs in Hitchcock's *Psycho*

(1960), in which the deftness of the cutting makes the woman who is murdered while showering appear to be nude when in fact she is never actually shown to be so—not even subliminally.

Actually, the film artist has all time and space at his disposal, as we have seen. If he wishes to root his camera to one spot, he can still turn it a full 360 degrees to show the entire horizon. Nor need he root the camera at all. He may move it along the terrain from spot to spot. Nor

Courtesy of Central Film Archives, Warsaw

Fig. 1. *Ashes* (1965). A canvas broadened.

need he even anchor it in time. All places, all times are available to his "canvas."

A film always transforms, surpasses, or recreates reality while it is recording it. Film is a medium and, because a medium expresses by means of its own qualities and colorations and has its own strengths and defects, it inevitably transforms what it attempts to represent. Cinema presumes a certain trust in the world as it is. Yet contrary to the old saw, the camera *does* "lie": it moves unexpectedly; it reduces dimensionality; it changes the natural size of an object or places it into an artificial context of juxtaposed or superimposed shots; it heightens a form by painting it with an unreal luminescence or beclouding it with an unreal darkness.

Far from being impassive, the camera must—if it is to maintain our interest—maintain a fluidity of space and time, which is often lacking in "reality." These devices and effects may be "lies," but they are some of the ways of art, and the means to improved perception.

Why is it that an argument so basic—and so obvious—explaining film as art has to be made? How is it that critics—those respected as such and those of self-generating reputations—have so often been blind to artistry in film when they grant it in other media? It is important to confront these questions, because film criticism itself has not only done much to foster quality in the movies, but has also done much to reduce it. In fact, few media are handled by a critical corps so fragmented and so much in basic conflict as is the cinema.

We begin with film history. Cinema was the first mass-entertainment art form to be invented in modern times. Literature, music, painting, sculpture, the dance, and the theater all had long, venerable traditions behind them when the first nickelodeons were in their heyday. Photography was also an invented art, of course, but it achieved nowhere near the popularity as an entertainment medium that its offspring, the moving pictures, amassed. The cinema was invented not by an artist, but by technicians. Completely mechanical, and astonishing in its effects, it had about it from the beginning an aura of being a wonder toy, and it focused on trivia. Even when it entered the world of art—capturing, for example, theatrical productions on film—it could offer only a poor, silent, flawed impression of the real thing. Furthermore, it was heavily shaped by its audience, which was the great mass public. In a short time, the movies became for the masses the staple of entertainment, and moviemakers quickly adjusted their productions to the common denominator of proletarian and middle-class tastes. And this, of course, meant that the movies quickly became big business, owned and operated not by artists or artistically minded entrepreneurs, but by businessmen—many of whom came to the new industry from completely different business backgrounds and whose interest was in giving the public only what it wanted.

That a film, for instance, such as *The Great Train Robbery* (1903) was a primitive but still noteworthy work of art, whose integrity should have been respected, did not occur to S. Lubin, who remade the film—virtually scene for scene and shot for shot—as a product to steal and sell. That *his* product still turned out inferior to Edwin Porter's original indicates the special quality a true artist can give to his work. Thus, while film makers—the budding directors, cameramen, and a few good actors—were making great strides in developing an art of film, and while some critics were coming to recognize this, those who owned the movies established a foundation of cheapness, commonness, and triviality.

Even as films were developing as an art, the movies had become a social institution and an industry, to be frowned upon by the world of art criticism. The theater might have its critics in the press, but the movies had gossip columnists. And these, of course, made no demands for quality film performances, but fed an insatiable public curiosity about the lives and follies of the "stars." The movies became a world with a culture unto itself. This world had its temples in the great movie palaces and its more modest chapels in the small, often slightly shabby neighborhood houses. It had its rituals—the "movie nights" that became family habits, and, of course, the Saturday afternoon movies for the kids. It had its hierarchy of gods and goddesses, from the great superstars to the ever-recurring and comfortably familiar character actors. Its mythology was gossip, sex scandals, and stories of meteoric rises to fame and fortune from humble beginnings. There were public crises over morals, there was the constant lure of Hollywood for the young, there were exotic stars from overseas, there were popcorn and bingo nights. There was, above all, the development of the most effective public relations and image-building apparatus ever seen. In the face of this pervasive movie culture, film art as such—at least as far as the public was concerned—remained remote and esoteric, and, naturally, in the face of this situation, the quality of film criticism suffered.

It still suffers, in part because film criticism seems specially vulnerable to cultural fads. And as a result, the simple truth that film is art—good or bad, as the case may be—is all too often denied or perverted. This can be seen in some of our "schools" of film criticism.

Pauline Kael has written that after seeing an art film, she wants to go out to a movie. We must suppose the art film was trash and we can only hope the movie was true art. Delight is after all a function of true art. For Miss Kael the art film means "artiness," and "artiness" may mean camera rhetoric for its own sake. There are film enthusiasts who take special pleasure in noting artful camera angles, curious cross-cuts, or other technically brilliant devices that make a film's rhetoric exciting. But is that enough? James Card, in assessing the work of William F. Adler, especially Adler's *The Second Coming* (1915), makes a necessary point:

Adler, by means which have defied all expert analysis or explanation, improvised some mysterious device which enabled his camera to follow action, to truck, dolly and zoom with sophisticated facility that seems often quite out of reach of many present-day studios so lavishly equipped with tracks, trucks, cranes, and lenses of variable focal length. The camera movement in *The Second Coming* makes ridiculous the measurement of moving camera shots in *The Birth of a Nation* and *Intolerance* for Adler makes camera mobility a primary technique rather than an exceptional device. The entire film is predominantly filled with full-screen close-ups. The picture is, of course, in its total effect, artless and quite devoid of content which could be considered of lasting interest.[3]

As Card suggests, camera technique, however brilliant, does not make a great movie. If artiness in a film irritates Miss Kael, we share her irritation.

Critics may also admire the setting, the splendid costumes, the excitement of physical combat, the style or personality of an actor, the musical score, or other facets of the film—for what pleasure these things create for them. But praising a movie solely for its bright colors or thrilling music or the jutting, dimpled chin of one of its actors is a form of self-indulgence. The object of any part of a good film or any good work of art is to contribute to the whole, and so such an appreciation really violates the point of a good film. It puts the viewer in the place of the object of his viewing.

Some critics commit the "historical fallacy" by equating old with classic. When Walker Allen said that he preferred silent films to talkies on grounds of "the less dialogue the better," he was letting nostalgia get in the way of his perception. To be a "classic" a film must carry its justification in every part—in fact in every shot—and it must transcend the conventions of its day.

While some critics limit their sights by nostalgia and antiquarianism, others are entrapped by an idolatry of stars or directors, fascinated by personal mystiques and private lives. Recently a more sophisticated group of critics has been coaxing journalism away from this cult of personality to a concern for the way directors reveal their personal style in their films. Evolved primarily among French critics at the *Cahiers du Cinéma,* this approach assumes that every good movie in a director's canon gains its value and impact solely from the single-minded plan or style which he imposes on actors and technicians in accordance with his "vision." The notion of a collection of dominant creative personalities hovering over, pervading, and unifying the total production of quality films has given rise to the phrase *"la politique des auteurs."* Consciously taking into account the whole historical and critical formation of cinema, especially in the work of "strong" American directors like Alfred Hitchcock, Howard Hawks, and John Ford, the *Cahiers* critics were able to illustrate this kind of authorial control by themselves becoming directors of New Wave (Nouvelle Vague) films. These directors, as did some earlier directors, listed their names as if they were, in fact, "authors": *Les Cousins* (1959) was *un film de* Claude Chabrol, as *David Copperfield* is a novel *by* Charles Dickens.

Cahiers critics have sought to establish credit for discovering particular technical devices. They praise Ernst Lubitsch for the jump-cut, Joseph von Sternberg for baroque adornment, and Alfred Hitchcock for visual rhythms. When they find no author evident in the film product, then, by implication, the movie is bad, often in spite of consistently excellent work by particular contributors. Thus Andrew Sarris, in judging a film such as Sidney Franklin's *The Good Earth* (1937), follows the *Cahiers* cataloguing system but makes his own judgments. He condemns the film as a totality because it fails to reflect an *auteur*'s policy, but he still praises the stars and the gimmicks that attracted the audience.[4] Pauline Kael, whose criticism is closely geared to her own personal response to a film, attacks the *auteur* theory on the grounds that its emphasis on one standard above all—the presence of the director's plan embodied throughout—leads *auteur* critics to praise bad films. Her view is sound—to a point, that point being the value that ambitious failure has always had in art, especially when the "failure" can be connected with an author's, a painter's, a composer's, or a director's total body of work.

Miss Kael's main criterion of value is perhaps just as arbitrary: the making of a significant social statement. In spite of the objections of such "humanistic" critics, the *auteur* theory remains exciting because it encourages the discovery and appreciation of genius—full-blown or developing. It uncovers the living artistic traditions that run through films and suggests the many possibilities of a personal directorial style. Finally, it focuses our attention on "pure" cinema, the film experience for its own sake as something to be judged, not for its cultural (political, social) contribution to society, but as quality of work within a medium. In short, what goes for Brueghel and Balzac and Britten ought to go for Antonioni, Kurosawa, and Ford.

The humanistic critics would argue that no film, and no contemporary work of art, whatever the age or the medium, can exist separately, and that this is especially so for that mass medium, the movies. Expression is propaganda: that fact is primary; the intensity of the propaganda—a film by Eisenstein as opposed, let us say, to a film by Lubitsch—is only a contributing factor. Thus Pauline Kael could like *L'Avventura* (1960), as socially and thematically moving, because it moved *her*, but rejected *La Notte* (1961) and *L'Eclisse* (1962), which completed Antonioni's trilogy, because they lacked the impact of the first. Naturally she has no sympathy for shoddy production, bad acting, or bad stories—she is a perceptive critic. But what marks a critic is not what he rejects so much as what he applauds—and why.

A third prominent school of film criticism pursues toughness of mind and sharpness of experience. These critics oppose the intellectualism of the *auteur* and humanist critics. The experience of film, so says Manny Farber, the chief exponent of this school, must be essential and total; judgmental criteria are only the results of word play. For the tough-guy critics, like Farber, the nickelodeon atmosphere, which survived into the 1930's in seamy little theaters like those lined up along New York's Forty-second Street, and which can still be found in all major cities, provides the proper milieu. The art house itself is, to them, anticinema, and the chief enemy to understanding film is pretension, be it present in the story, in the actor's gestures, or in directorial "artiness." To these critics it follows that films of "moral uplift," like those of Stanley Kramer, performers who "overact," like Bette Davis, and even, perhaps, a figure such as Orson Welles who "overdirected" *Citizen Kane* (1941), are fair game for condemnation. For Harold Clurman, the chief image of the movies of the thirties is "a punch in the jaw." Whether in physical action or pointed speech, the chief virtue of film lies in direct communication.

The very history of film has encouraged the evolution of these theories. The *auteur* theory stems from the fact that ever since the first directors decided where to place their cameras for greatest effect, the director has acted as an *auteur*, setting up policies of filming, acting, and even narration. He may work in conjunction with other artists and technicians and may even defer to their judgment; but the final decisions, the final policy are his, and this has been true from Porter, Méliès, and Griffith through Fellini, Resnais, and Kramer. The crux is, what value judgments should this fact of history and artistic organization call forth?

The humanistic bias stems from the nature of our age itself, and from the emphasis that socially involved artists have placed upon the mass media as ways of influencing our way of life for the better. In the twentieth century—as in the nineteenth—all art forms have been used for their ability to move their audiences to action or belief. Picasso's *Guernica*, Brecht's *The Jewish Woman* and *Man Is Man*, John Latouche and Earl Robinson's *Ballad for Americans*, Émile Zola's *Germinal*, the unremembered radio plays of Norman Corwin, these are but a smattering from other art forms that have had as their intent the dissemination of socially significant themes. Before the vogue of television, no medium was more widespread in intense following than the movies. Robert Sherwood's *The Petrified Forest* spoke its powerful message to many thousands as a play on Broadway (1934), but as a movie (1936) it touched millions. Not only do the great social issues of our day call for constant treatment, but it has also seemed natural that the heaviest responsibility for doing this should have been placed on the film. Some of the greatest films ever made have been intended as propaganda, but other great films have been thematically *dégagé* or simply wrongheaded in their themes. The humanistic critic must also recognize criteria having nothing to do with thematic significance.

The old nostalgia never burns down, it merely shifts its focus. The tough-minded criticism of Farber, Clurman, and others of their position is at heart nostalgia and a misreading of cinema as an institution and an art form. Farber and Clurman are right when they maintain that for many millions the essential film experience is a simple, direct, and unpretentious thing. The Indian biting the dust, the sock in the jaw (anybody's jaw), the pie in the face (in the case of Cagney, read "grapefruit"), the bullet in the gut, the bomb in the building have jolted audiences all over the world, as have sharp, direct dialogue and simple, naïve stories. Producers and those who work for them have amassed fortunes by turning out films which, for all their length, color, wideness of screen, stereophonicity of sound, and thousands of cast, retain the essential spirit of the nickelodeon. The twenties and thirties had a special and often exciting aura. Even to critics too young to have known that storied time, the thirties—those years in which so many stars "were born"—may have a romantic attraction. The special glamour of Hollywood on one side and the gloom of the neighborhood movie house on the other offer colorations too tantalizing to be ignored. But is this a value of film or a value of personal psychology? And, considering the universe of films that has been made, can we truly say that that is all there is to film?

Film is rich enough as an art to allow all three theories to coexist. Just as the aesthetics of literature traditionally invites variety and controversy regarding its methods and ·aims, so do theories of film. What is crucial is that we avoid oversimplifying the film experience. To be alert to the full richness of concept and technique that makes a good film is to elevate the cinema to its rightful place in our culture. To know how films are made, to know how the film maker moves us, entices us, jolts us, and brings us to tears, not only with sentiments but with a host of means to project sheer beauty before us, is to make the seeing of a film much more of an adventure and, if the film is truly good, a triumph. To like what one likes is to make a valid judgment about art; but to seek to know *why* one likes art that is well wrought is to open oneself to a broader, richer world of sensitivity and perception.

The expansion of perception and of the capacity to taste fully of the film experience is the aim of this book.

AIM.

CHAPTER TWO

Continuity

How did early film makers discover what was right for the screen? They knew that in arcades pictures of Sandow the Strong Man would entice a penny from boys who wanted to see him flex his muscles. They knew that the excitement of seeing motion actually reproduced on film attracted crowds. They showed filmed vaudeville sketches and magic shows because crowds loved vigorous and exotic physical activity. Eventually two kinds of film would dominate the screen: the peep show and the chase. As primitive tribes described them to Hortense Powder-maker, "kiss-kiss" and "bang-bang" stories are right for the screen.[1]

What *was* right *is* right: peep shows and chases still attract audiences. The lure of the peep-show element is its forbidden or private nature. When a character is about to go to the race track, the director shows him changing his trousers as he receives a tip on a horse. A girl going out with an older man against her mother's wishes, as in Joseph L. Mankiewicz' *Letter to Three Wives* (1948), is putting on her stockings and straightening seams while she argues with her mother. The gaudy bathing scenes in films by Cecil B. De Mille are examples of the peep show made lavish. The kinds and settings of chases are abundant. Cowboys chase Indians; hunters chase animals (and vice versa); cops, robbers; indignant citizens, monsters; aquanauts, fish. Chases take place through fire, in outer space, under water, along the rim of the earth. Rooftops, deserts, marshes with patches of quicksand, roller coasters, merry-go-rounds, the sides of skyscrapers and ledges, the Statue of Liberty (Hitchcock's *Saboteur*, 1942), Mount Rushmore (his *North by Northwest*, 1959), ice floes (D. W. Griffith's *Way Down East*, 1920, and Andrzej Wajda's *Ashes*, 1965), frozen lakes (Sergei

15

Eisenstein's *Alexander Nevsky*, 1938, and Gian Luigi Polidoro's *To Bed or Not to Bed*, 1964), around giant clocks (Harold Lloyd), and on top of locomotives (Buster Keaton's *The General*, 1926)—these have all been settings for chases. For farce the chases could be speeded up; for melodrama, as in dreams of helplessness, slowed down. The precision with which the director was able to reproduce the tempo of athletes chasing each other or a ball or of dancers following each other in a chorus line made the baseball story and the musical right for the screen. Even Alain Resnais' *Last Year at Marienbad* (1962) uses peep shows and chases, in this instance for the surrealistic expression of complex ideas about time, memory, and social alienation: the camera pursues through lonely corridors, analogous to the avenues of the mind, the identity of a moment of time. Film makers have the ability to think creatively in terms of moving pictures. The peep-show and chase elements can be so attenuated that sublime thought and complex feeling overshadow the vulgarity that at one time seemed to dominate the screen.

Although right for the screen, peep shows and chases are, in a sense, protonarrative elements. Simple movements in film, like the cowboy mounting his horse, the gangster driving into a filling station and performing a hold-up, dancers kicking high in a chorus line, and soldiers charging out of trenches—all kinesthetic actions—must in fictional films also serve to advance a story. Brutal actions or excruciatingly slow tortures reach the nervous system of the spectator in horror films and in war stories with patriotic or pacifist intentions. The essence of storytelling in cinema lies in the fact that pictures and sound will be used to show characters "doing and suffering," as Aristotle says, and either changing their environment or being changed by it. With picture and sound, the cinematic storyteller exhibits a single unified plot through which he affects the emotions of the moviegoer and enables him to participate in a ritual such as, for example, theater and poetry are thought always to provide.

The making of a movie may *begin* with a story idea, presented by an agent to a potential producer. The producer may then assign scriptwriters to compose a scenario, or working script, but before the director begins the film, he often prepares, or has an artist prepare, a "storyboard." A storyboard is concerned, however, with more than story or plot; it is the director's attempt to outline his story pictorially stage by stage. It consists of a "book" in which he pastes drawings of characters in various locations. Below each picture he designates which stage of the story this represents or the dialogue that accompanies it and whether the shot will be most effective as a close-up, middle shot, or long shot (as well as any other feelings about the camera setup that occur to him).* He may note which shots are to consist merely of stock footage to be taken from the studio library. The following storyboard used for Allan Dwan's *The Sands of Iwo Jima* (1949) shows how a film's action and plot are visually conceived.

First we have the artist's conception of the landing party in their boat, with directions for a superimposed process plate that will suggest weather conditions and time of day (Fig. 2a). Room for a shot to be taken entirely from the studio's library is indicated by the blank space that follows (Fig. 2b). The artist then conceives of the establishing shot for the battle (actually to be filmed at Camp Pendleton, California, rather than on Iwo Jima) as a long shot (Fig. 2c). As the notation indicates, the director will have the camera dolly in along with the landing

Fig. 2. Section of a storyboard for *The Sands of Iwo Jima* (1949).

Courtesy of Repix, Inc.

Fig. 2a. Scene 117-B

X117A. PROCESS PLATE TO COVER.

117B. INT. AMTRAC: SHOOTING ASTERN (PROCESS) Stryker comes on to Conway.

Fig. 2b. Scene 117-C. Stock

X117B. PROCESS PLATE TO COVER.

117C. BATTLE ACTION (STOCK).

Fig. 2c. Scene 117-D, as *drawn*

117D. EXT. BEACH: (LONG) (CAMP PENDLETON)
The beach is littered with wreckage. . . . More Amtracs are coming in.
CAMERA DOLLIES with our squad's Amtrac until it hits the beach. . . .

* Moviemakers think of distances on screen in terms of what the camera reveals of the human body, the close-up being from the shoulders to top of head; the close middle shot, a bust shot; the middle shot, known in foreign criticism as the "American" shot, from the knees up; the full shot includes the whole body; the long shot, the whole body and some details of the set; and the far shot, or very long shot, a distant background as well as the setting.

craft. Below the drawing and script excerpt is the still from the completed filming of this scene (Fig. 2d).

Having established the broad canvas of the battle, the artist indi-

Fig. 2d. Scene 117-D, as *filmed*

cates details of the action: a medium low-angle shot of the disembarkment (Fig. 2e), followed by a close "two-shot" of men still in the boat (Fig. 2f). A new establishing shot prepares for the battle on the beach (Fig. 2g). The artist illustrates the ensuing action in a series of draw-

Fig. 2e. Scene 118

Fig. 2f. Scene 119

Fig. 2g. Scene 120

118. EXT. BEACH: MED. AMTRAC SHOOTING FROM LOW ANGLE. Lt. Baker starts over side.

119. EXT. BEACH: CLOSE
Stryker and Bass.

120. EXT. BEACH:
A coconut log revetment runs along the sand. . . . Marines of the first wave are crouched behind it. An Amtrac with a gaping hole in its side veers crazily. . . .

ings alternating between close-up and middle-foreground views of some of the principal characters (Figs. 2h, i, j). The final film form of Fig. 2j of the storyboard—the Marines looking from the revetment "further down the beach" (Fig. 2k)—crystallizes the artist's drawing but shows through the fifth man in the picture the modification that emerges during the

Fig. 2h. Scene 128D

128D. EXT. BEACH: CLOSE Stryker.

Fig. 2i. Scene 129

129. EXT. BEACH: MED. Stryker and the squad are in the foreground. . . . Intense background action. Captain Joyce . . . crawls down the beach and stops near Stryker.

Fig. 2j. Scene 129A

129A. EXT. BEACH: CLOSE Stryker and Captain Joyce, other men of the squad in background.

Fig. 2k. *Filmed* version of Scene 129A (Fig. 2j)

actual filming: the fifth man is absorbed with some danger he senses.

Two of the sketches for another sequence in *The Sands of Iwo Jima* (Figs. 2l and m) show the progress of the battle, and a third (Fig. 2n)— a reaction shot—registers the fatigue engendered by this activity. By varying day and night scenes of battle (stock shots from any similar battle

Fig. 2l. Scene 145A

145A. . . . their bayonets gleaming. Hellenopolis is killed.

Fig. 2m. Scene 149A

149A. The Captain starts to get to his feet, preparatory to dashing across to Bass. A mortar shell strikes driving him back. Stryker points his M1 rifle at him.

Fig. 2n. Scene 149B

149B. The CAMERA MOVES SLOWLY IN until Stryker's grim tortured face is in EXTREME CLOSE-UP.

will be accepted in the minds of the audience as shots of the Battle of Iwo Jima), the director will show the passage of time pictorially (Fig. 2-o). Finally the artist sets up the last sequence of the film with a middle-foreground drawing of columns of victorious troops (Fig. 2p), followed by three closely linked details: the Marine's off-screen gaze, known as a *look of outward regard* (Fig. 2q), anticipates an *eye-line shot* of what he sees (Fig. 2r), which in turn signals the *reaction shot* that ends the

Fig. 2-o. Scene 151. Stock shots

151. EXT. TARAWA: (DAY AND NIGHT SHOTS) (STOCK) SHOTS of the battle as it progresses. Over the shots we hear various voices.

Fig. 2p. Scene 152

152. EXT. ISLAND ROAD: (DAY) FULL Moving line of Marines. They come past the camera; their blackened faces mirror complete exhaustion.

film (Fig. 2s), the Marine lowering his eyes because he was not the first to raise the flag.

The storyboard artist, guided by the director, captures the actions and passions that will be translatable into film, varying throughout the camera distances and angles that will evoke surprise or pathos. Even

Fig. 2q. Scene 152A	Fig. 2r. Scene 153	Fig. 2s. Scene 154
152A. . . . As Ragazzi comes past the camera, he looks up at something off screen.	153. EXT. TRUNK OF PALM TREE: At the top of the trunk, all the foliage of which has been blasted off by shellfire, an American flag waves in the breeze.	154. EXT. ISLAND ROAD: CLOSE Ragazzi. As he lowers his eyes again, he mutters to himself. "Somebody beat me to it."

though his series of drawings is accompanied by written actions and dialogue, the continuity, reminiscent of action comic strips, remains primarily pictorial. After the film is shot according to the plan of the storyboard, the film editor, sometimes with the director or the producer or both, undertakes both the final cutting and the assembling of the filmstrips into the whole.

In fictional films the word *story* is therefore not quite accurate. *Story* belongs to the phases before production when film makers in conference describe in words to one another what they will show on the screen, or when they write summaries of their plots as *story ideas*, *scenarios*, and *scripts*. It refers also to the narratives we tell one another after we have seen a film, as well as to postproduction scripts like the published versions of Ingmar Bergman's screenplays or the one of Tony Richardson's *Tom Jones*. As the storyboard suggests, a film maker tells his "story" through a succession of shots. Therefore, more accurate than *story* is the word <u>continuity</u>, which acknowledges that picture and sound grouped together as shots, rather than written words alone, are the means of cinematic storytelling. A film is made ordinarily in segments, not necessarily in its final shot order. The director's task is to make each shot as good as he can and later to assemble all shots into an effective order, to give the film its continuity.

As an example of continuity we could use any film, but let us take a "classic," James Whale's *Frankenstein* (1931). Its excellence cannot be judged solely by Mary Shelley's novel or by Boris Karloff's impersonation of the Monster or by its theme or camera work. The chief criterion is Whale's skill in mounting a collection of shots that contain pictorial accords and oppositions. Other criteria, though necessary for the full cinematic experience, are encompassed within this key factor, since they are contributions to the total narrative effect.

Whale opens with pictures of a cemetery at night: in the first shot, the camera travels across a misty area covered with dark foliage; it discovers a grave and a body being buried. The director tries to arouse fear by the sound of earth falling on the coffin, by a lap dissolve* to the completed grave and by a shot of its subsequent reopening by Dr. Frankenstein and his hunchbacked assistant. Among the *mise en scène* (details of setting) are a hanging, swaying skeleton in a medical lecture hall; surgical instruments used for dissection—shown in close-up; disembodied brains, one marked "normal," the other "abnormal," the topic of a medical lecture; Dr. Frankenstein's private laboratory, and particularly a table, on which a sewn-together body, the sutures visible on its neck and wrist, is raised toward an open roof to receive lightning that will generate life in it. Finally, the fluttering eyelids of the awakening Monster signal the awesome climax of these terrifying sequences.

The camera angles are sharp; scenes are rarely photographed from normal angles of vision. The pan shot† becomes a source of fright—what new horror will the camera discover?—as when the camera pans from a child playing with flowers to bushes in which we see the enlarged eyes of the approaching Monster.

When Whale shoots daytime scenes, ablaze with sunlight, or restores normal camera angles, his obvious purpose is to provide contrasts with the horror to come. Bavarian peasant dances in costume, supposedly representative of simple mountain life, are interrupted and intercut with the horror of the Monster and a child dropping flowers into a lake and watching them float. Later the child's father interrupts the gaiety, as he carries the dead girl across the sunlit square.

---

* In a lap dissolve a second shot is gradually superimposed upon the scene being projected, as it, in turn, slowly "dissolves" or diminishes.

† A pan shot is achieved when the camera shoots while swinging on its vertical axis, its base remaining stationary. The term is derived from *panoramic* because with this motion the camera can easily explore a distant panorama, encompassing 360 degrees of the horizon if necessary.

In addition to establishing horror by details of *mise en scène* and by contrasts, Whale complicates the emotion we feel by including details that arouse pity for the Monster, so that we cannot entirely triumph in his destruction. The Monster is shown to share with fellow humans a fear of fire, the element that ultimately destroys him. He arouses our pity when he is bound in a cellar and whipped or burned by Dr. Frankenstein's assistant, Fritz. He also appears to have a capacity for love and pleasure, as in his playing with the child and the flowers. His face as shown in the close-ups that alternate with middle-distance shots sometimes appears to be troubled, for he cannot understand the world he lives in or his own motivations.

The Faustian theme, perennial in science fiction, is that of a scientist's successful attempt to recreate life in dead bodies. It carries the anti-intellectual lesson that there are areas of knowledge in which man has no right to experiment. The wise man, according to this theme, leaves unanswered certain questions about the source of life. James Whale, happily, omits the church ending usual in such films—the sermon which concludes that some questions are the province of God. Instead, he is content to have given us a continuity of shots which lead us from suspense, to terror, to pity.

While it is true that the film maker has verbal means at his disposal, the filmgoer expects him to tell the story largely in terms of moving pictures. A moviegoer will be tolerant of words, but grows bored when the pictures are not the primary means of storytelling. As Erwin Panofsky points out, the "price the cinema has to pay" for visual storytelling is that both actions and inner states of mind, or philosophy, must be "spatialized."[2] Hamlet can *say* he is going to England, and the playgoer is content. In a film, however, the director must *show* the passage of time, making time visual, that is, by making objects move in space. For example, after a character says he is going to Los Angeles, the filmgoer expects to see an airplane in flight or some familiar Los Angeles landmark coming into view. The film maker shows the passage of time not only with the legend "Argonne Forest, 1918" but also with the physical action of cannon firing or troops leaving trenches to fight. Words are not enough. The passage of time must be shown through changed spatial relations—an object must change its position in relation to its background or to the limits of the frame. In like manner the moviegoer is not content to have a scene remain static or frozen for any length of time. If objects, architecture, or any aspects of setting are immobile by nature, the spectator at least expects the camera to move in relation ıem, or he hopes to view them from different distances and angles ın a series of dynamic "cuts."

When a moviegoer remains preoccupied with dialogue, remaining literary-conscious rather than shot-conscious, he ends by looking at a window as if it were a wall. Consider the ways in which the art of the film is both different from and similar to certain literary genres in the way it fashions a story. Between movies and the stage there are fundamental differences which go to the heart of each medium. In theater the basic division of action is the scene, whether determined by a particular setting or time span, or, as in the French style, by the entrance or exit of characters. In a film, however, the fundamental unit is the shot, or single camera operation, a great number of which may actually combine to form a "sequence," that is, in the stage sense, a scene. For example, in the theater two men may talk in a law office in a scene taking twenty minutes. In a film, on the other hand, this same scene might consist of a sequence of fifty shots. The first might be a middle shot of the two men in profile facing each other, the second might focus on the face of the first man and the back of the second, the third might be a close-up (or detail) of a coffee cup on the desk, and so on.

Good film makers compose sequences out of such a variety of shots not merely, as many believe, for the sake of giving a continual flow of fresh sensations to the eye of the spectator. Their main aim is to heighten visual perceptions of meaning, feeling, and form. In the law office scene the camera cuts to the face of the speaker or listener whose outward emotional reaction is more dramatic, and then to the image of the cup to stress an important—possibly a symbolic—detail. Furthermore, the camera may "look down" upon one character from above and "look up" to the other from below—this is, as we shall see, one of the many simple ways in which the film maker, unlike the dramatist, can directly indicate an "attitude" toward his subject.

Indeed, the possibility of constantly varying the position and focus of the camera plus the ability to cut rapidly from shot to shot is what most distinguishes the art of the film from the theater and places it closer to the novel. D. W. Griffith, as a matter of fact, admitted that he was able to devise two of the most vital elements in the grammar of film—close-ups and cross-cuts*—only after a careful study of Dickens. One need merely glance at the opening pages of *Great Expectations* to

* In a cross-cut the director switches to another action, that is, juxtaposes another shot, then cuts back to the original action.

see that a fluid "camera point of view" is operative: a middle shot of the cemetery moves into a close-up of the gravestones, and then pans the landscape in long shot. Later Dickens provides a "subjective" camera view of the swinging church steeple when Pip is turned upside down by Magwitch.* Since craftsmanship delimits emotion, such devices—varying camera distances and point of view—in both Dickens and Griffith often actually control what appears, on the mere narrative level of their work, to be undisciplined sentimentality.

Like the novelist, the film maker is free to manipulate time as well as distance and space. Violations of normal time sequences, as in the "flash back" and the "flash forward,"† and alternations between parallel actions are of course possible in the theater, but protraction or compression of a scene by restructuring its fragments is not. Let us say it takes an actor in reality ten seconds to cross a room (or stage). A film editor can condense this to three seconds by "jump-cutting" from the initial segment of the action to its concluding segment. Or he may prolong the time by joining together a series of "overlap" shots; that is, each of several shots of the action (from different angles) will repeat part of the distance covered in the previous shot. Another way of extending time is to represent serially the simultaneously occurring details of an action, as Eisenstein does in the famous Odessa Steps massacre in *Potemkin* (1925) when he "analyzes" the tableau into details of Cossacks' boots and the wheels of a runaway baby carriage, along with

---

* The opening paragraphs of *Great Expectations*, in which Pip is the narrator, run as follows:

". . . I found out for certain that this bleak place overgrown with nettles was the churchyard; and that Philip Pirrip, late of this parish, and also Georgiana wife of the above, were dead and buried; and that Alexander, Bartholomew, Abraham, Tobias, and Roger, infant children of the aforesaid, were also dead and buried; and that the dark flat wilderness beyond the churchyard, intersected with dykes and mounds and gates, with scattered cattle feeding on it, was the marshes; and that the low leaden line beyond was the river; and that the distant savage lair from which the wind was rushing, was the sea. . . .

"The man, after looking at me for a moment, turned me upside down, and emptied my pockets. There was nothing in them but a piece of bread. When the church came to itself—for he was so sudden and strong that he made it go head over heels before me, and I saw the steeple under my feet—when the church came to itself, I say, I was seated on a high tombstone, trembling, while he ate the bread ravenously." (*Great Expectations*, New York: Rinehart and Co., 1960, p. 2.)

S. M. Eisenstein was the first to elaborate on Griffith's indebtedness to Dickens. See his "Dickens, Griffith, and the Film Today," *Film Form* (New York: Meridian Books, 1957), pp. 195-255.

† A "flash forward" is an anticipatory shot of a future scene which recurs later in its normal time sequence. It usually represents a speculation about the future in the mind of a character, as in the mind of Diego (Yves Montand) in Resnais' *La Guerre Est Finie* (1966).

Fig. 3a

Fig. 3b

Fig. 3c

Fig. 3. *Potemkin* (1925). "Odessa Steps sequence." Establishing shot of Cossack massacre (Fig. 3a) and its "analysis" by means of two details (Figs. 3b and 3c).

reaction shots of an old woman with glasses and of a mother with a dead child (Fig. 3). Both "overlapping" and "analyzing" impose a view and rhythm of experience quite different from the order of actuality, or that of the stage.

From this it can be seen that the further one penetrates to the heart of cinematic structure and movement the nearer one comes to discovering something that is very much like poetry. Intercutting or juxtaposing shots of different material (what Eisenstein calls "montage") sets up visual similes and metaphors, as in a poem. A famous example is the way in which Eisenstein in *Strike* (1924) intercuts shots of a bull being slaughtered with details of the brutal handling of a mob. Sometimes a close-up of an object can make it a poetic symbol, as the stress on hands tends to do in Frank Perry's *David and Lisa* (1962), and the repetition of a device, like the "zoom-freezes"* of the face of the dead father in Tony Richardson's *Loneliness of the Long Distance Runner* (1962) or the "wanted" posters in François Truffaut's *400 Blows* (1959), creates a type of rhyme or refrain.

The recognition of such poetic elements in a film is ultimately the only valid way for a moviegoer to be "literary-minded." Should he praise the story of *The Last Laugh* (1924), he should also point out how the sense of the old doorman's tragedy is enhanced by the gradual shift of the camera angle from low to high, or how photographing him through the hotel's perpetually revolving door reveals the fast tempo of the world which will crush him. Every movie sequence is like a deck of picture cards, and the significance of a film experience lies in the arrangement of shots. The alert filmgoer who is interested in story must become shot-oriented, aware of moving forms and moving camera, of angles, of contrasts between foregrounds and backgrounds, of playing areas of the screen in which actors are placed.

Cinematic continuity also requires a pictorialized cause-effect relationship. E. M. Forster says of fiction that the sentence, "The king died and the queen died," is a story; but that the causal statement, "Because the king died, the queen also died," is a plot.[3] In order to convey a simple story in pictures, without words, the film maker must show the king, perhaps on a bed, with a servant closing his eyes, and then being borne to a tomb. But how can he show the plot? Perhaps the same three shots could be intercut with the queen looking forlornly at the bed where the king is lying, and then in tears as the servant closes his eyes,

---

* In a zoom-freeze the photographed action is suddenly brought from far away to close-up by an adjustment of the camera lens and is then halted or frozen into a "still."

and finally dejectedly walking in his funeral procession. Then the queen can be shown to die by means of the same sequence of three shots with parallel settings and camera movements. In a novel or play words are sufficient, and sometimes in a movie they are satisfactory. But the moviegoer expects to see actions and the chain of reactions they set off rather than exclusively to be told about them.

As Francis Fergusson points out, all dramatic action is primarily that of the psyche or soul.[4] This is what novels and plays share with film. Although the stories in film genres like the western and the thriller are, of course, less exalted than the work of Sophocles, simple quest stories often involve the action and reaction of the psyche. The western hero avenging his father's death or Sam Spade (Humphrey Bogart) in John Huston's *The Maltese Falcon* (1941) seeking his partner's murderer advances through suspense-making physical and moral adventures toward a confrontation and a denouement. The episodes through which he proceeds cannot be reversed, as in episodic plots, which lack causality: once Sam Spade learns of the murder of his partner and announces that a detective whose partner's murder is unsolved is allowing something that is "bad for business," he cannot be deterred from his work in spite of "the Fat Man" (Sidney Greenstreet), Peter Lorre, Elisha Cook, Jr., or Mary Astor; he may seem to become interested in the money and the adventuress, but his purpose goes by the most direct route to its fulfillment. As in *Oedipus Rex*, the plot in *The Maltese Falcon* follows a causal sequence during which a series of probable events leads to the confrontation of all the possible murderers and to the denouement, at which Mary Astor, rejected by Bogart, rides down the elevator in police custody, the bars of the sliding elevator door casting shadows on her face, as if she were already in prison.

Probability within a causal sequence remains the chief feature of any good plot. The organic nature of continuity requires that probability—the necessity that what is most likely to happen in given circumstances, rather than what is freakishly possible, should happen—be maintained throughout a film. Foreshadowing is both a fictional and a cinematic device that elevates the merely possible to the probable. Because it is now a historical fact, the assassination of President Kennedy is of course "possible," but from the point of view of art it is "improbable." When Bruce Conner gives the event a continuity (see p. 4), he gives it probability.

In order for an event to be probable in art, the audience requires knowledge, or hints, of antecedent actions and motivations of character.

For example, in Carol Reed's *The Third Man* (1949), pictures of a cat licking a boot in a doorway prepare the moviegoer for the knowledge that Harry Lime (Orson Welles) is alive. Without such preparation, the "resurrection" of Lime would be improbable. In *Citizen Kane* (1941), which turns on the question, "Who is 'Rosebud'?"—Kane's last word—the meaning is subtly planted before the probable denouement. The snow scene in the glass ball that the dying Kane drops after he utters the name "Rosebud" is followed in a later sequence by an actual snow scene in which the boy Kane is playing with his sled. When the boy, who is reluctant to leave with Thatcher, hits the older man in the stomach with the sled, the viewer glimpses the trade-mark of a rosebud on the sled. (Orson Welles, as director, is careful, however, not to reveal the written word *Rosebud*, which is also on the sled, until the end of the film.) As the boy leaves his farm, a long, detailed shot shows the sled piling up with snow, its trade-mark and name again hidden. As the boy later unwraps a Christmas present, he rejects the gift of a sled—it is *not Rosebud*. These visual clues, known fully only in retrospect, make the film's continuity probable. At the end of the film, the sled with the name *Rosebud* burns among the effects left behind by Kane, signaling the detour in Kane's life that has taken him from his mother's boarding-house, where he might have flourished emotionally. It is as if Kane as a boy knew intuitively what was best for him, and as if his parents and guardians were working against his nature, or psyche, to convert him to what he could not be.

The film maker has cinematic means not only for establishing but also for reversing the probable line of a film's story, especially when he wants dramatic irony. For example, when Kane is running for political office, his success is threatened by his opponent's having discovered him to be keeping a woman in a love nest. Kane's powerful personality and his assertion that he will win anyway arouse the confidence of the audience. Still the viewer knows, from previous accounts of the Kane story, that in politics Kane is "destined to be a bridesmaid but never a bride." However, the director, Welles, follows the shot concerned with the love nest with a close-up of a newspaper headline: "Kane Elected." Since important events of a film's plot are conventionally shown in newspaper headlines, the audience for the moment expects that Kane has won. But Welles at this point draws the camera back from the headline to reveal that the news sheet is still in the press—that of the *Inquirer*, owned by Kane. The increased camera distance also reveals Bernstein reading this headline and saying of another headline, "Kane Defeated,

Fraud at Polls" (that we also see), "I guess we'll have to print that one." Kane has lost the election, in accordance with the audience's original expectation, which has been temporarily reversed. Thus Welles establishes a probable story and toys with its ironic reversal, using an increased camera distance to effect it.

The cinema has been so varied in creating such reversals, the basis of one important kind of excitement in filmgoing, that advertisers frequently use the word "suspense" to urge filmgoers into theaters. Suspense in the movies is conventionally thought to lie in chases, as when the good men ride after the cattle rustlers, who seem to be momentarily triumphant. The intercut, from one group to another, or, in a fist fight, from one antagonist to the other, is the usual method for delaying the outcome of the action. But a film maker has other means to make us expectant of what the camera will find. When Kane's mistress suffers through her operatic debut at the Chicago Opera House, the camera reaches, like the singer after her high note, toward the upper parts of the house. It passes from the singer on stage upward past the flies and comes to rest on two stage hands on a catwalk, one of whom comments on the quality of the singing by holding his nose.

All techniques in cinematic storytelling that prolong the time of an action create suspense, as we have seen in our examples of an increased camera distance (the newspaper headlines), of the crane shot (in the opera house), or of the intercut (as in a conventional chase). Suspense delays the logical consequence in the development of a causal sequence. Time, however, must not be prolonged to the degree that it interferes with the unified whole, overtaxing the attention span of the audience. Proportion requires that time be prolonged, but not distorted. Boredom results from such disproportion. When the camera does not locate the center of interest or when it dwells over insignificant or meaningless detail, not connected to the continuity, the filmgoer will be tempted to leave the theater.

Sometimes, however, the material found by the searching camera only appears to lack significance or is of such an order of thought that it merely seems meaningless. Those addicted to causal sequences of action films sometimes find the stress of an avant-garde director whose shots do not fall into a conventionally logical pattern to be without one. Agnes Varda's Le Bonheur (1966) seems merely to repeat instances in which a man feels happiness, as he walks among flowers, surrounded by the wife and children or the mistress he loves. He sleeps, he makes love; and all the props stress a happiness in simplicity. The conflict in the film lies in what is unstated. While all the images prepare the filmgoer for accepting a conventional happiness, the theme that emerges from the succession of "happy" scenes is that the "happy" life is not worth living. All the insignificant materials are, in fact, part of a causal sequence whose suspense lies in the spectator's gradual awareness that what he is seeing is, in fact, deplorable: the denouement, the suicide of the wife and her replacement by a mistress who will become a second wife of the happy man, does not lead the hero to self-knowledge, to an awareness of a false ideal. The spectator, left however with a set of shots that convey a complex philosophical thought, must supply to the images received the principle that organizes what he has seen.

Cinematic devices enable a plot to be told in a continuity of shots, but they also enable the film maker to show probable people performing the actions of the plot. Since the configuration of the plot is in fact determined by how characters act and think, the film maker must find cinematic devices for delineating them. He has, of course, verbal and narrative means at his disposal—dialogue, sketches by other characters, and the like. The film maker, however, is also a pictorial artist who can use the distortion techniques of the caricaturist for sharpening character: a close low-angle shot of Sidney Greenstreet's stomach in *The Maltese Falcon* emphasizes the fat man's overpowering greed; the famous low-angle long shot of Jedediah (Joseph Cotten) through the towering legs of Kane in the foreground establishes the tyranny of the latter over the former. In these instances the director is using actors as props in order to reveal the personalities of the characters they portray. He may also highlight the performer's acting talent in close shots that make the human face an instrument for conveying inner feelings. Sensuality is, perhaps, the easiest emotion. It may be conveyed by wet, parted lips. In Erich von Stroheim's *Greed* (1924) Tina bites her own forefinger or glows ecstatically over gold coins to show the sublimation of her sexual passion into miserliness. In silent films emotions tended to be conventionalized in what we may call libretto acting: shyness conveyed by a finger at the chin or villainy by a face contorted into a snarl or the twirling of mustaches. Such gestures were broad. Characterization may lie in less obvious arrangement of the actor's features, as in the enigmatic face of Garbo that ends Rouben Mamoulian's *Queen Christina* (1933) or Robert Mitchum's highlighted eyebrows as he calls the children hiding in the cellar in Charles Laughton's *The Night of the Hunter* (1955): "Children! . . . I can feel myself gettin' awful mad, children." In *October* (1928) Eisenstein simply cross-cut Kerensky and a peacock to characterize the interim leader of the Russian Revolution.

A remarkable fact about the history of screen stories is that in sixty years the medium has found essentially nonverbal methods of presenting plot, character, and thought, elements that function organically in a unique art form. Using pictures exclusively, Andrzej Wajda can ask a philosophical question. In *Samson* (1961), the story of a Warsaw Jew between 1939 and 1944, the hero follows the procession of Jews being marched to the ghetto. Still outside, he sees a wooden fence being constructed; the other Jews are behind it. The following shots (Fig. 4) show the fence in construction. The last shot of the sequence will show the final board hammered into the fence with a little cross on the corner. The question Wajda asks by showing the shape of the cross that becomes a confining wall concerns the responsibility of Christians toward Jewish martyrs—an abstract thought, potentially a cliché, is thus presented nonverbally, and yet is an eloquent, passionate pictorial statement.

The cinematic storyteller, as we have seen, has at his disposal picto-

Fig. 4. *Samson* (1961). A pictorial statement of a philosophical question: a cross becomes a fence. (The first of this series was not used in the final version.)

From Wajda's Workbooks. Courtesy of Central Film Archives, Warsaw

Fig. 4a

Fig. 4b

Fig. 4d

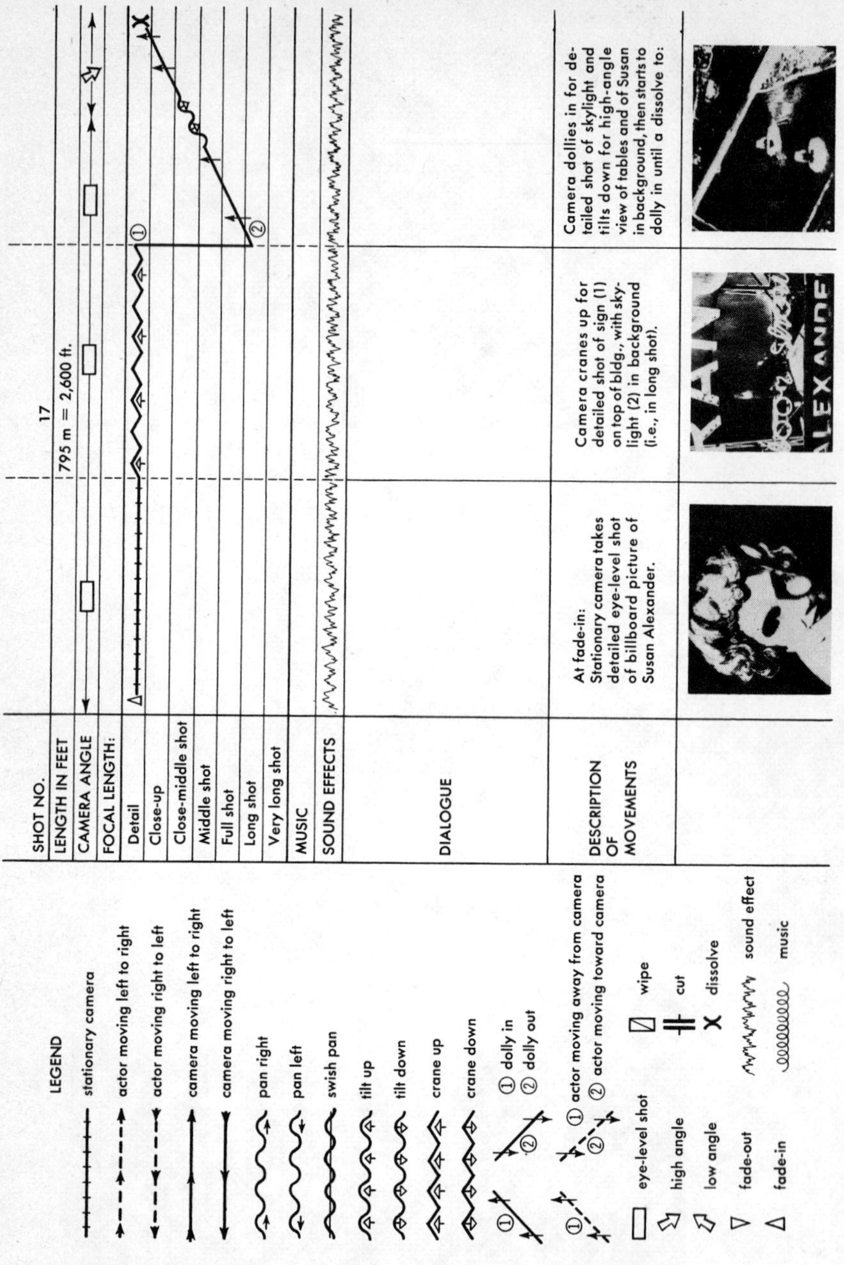

LEGEND

- stationary camera
- actor moving left to right
- actor moving right to left
- camera moving left to right
- camera moving right to left
- pan right
- pan left
- swish pan
- tilt up
- tilt down
- crane up
- crane down
- ① dolly in ② dolly out
- ① actor moving away from camera ② actor moving toward camera
- eye-level shot
- high angle
- low angle
- fade-out
- fade-in
- wipe
- cut
- dissolve
- sound effect
- music

SHOT NO.	17		
LENGTH IN FEET	795 m = 2,600 ft.		
CAMERA ANGLE			
FOCAL LENGTH: Detail			
Close-up			
Close-middle shot			
Middle shot			
Full shot			
Long shot			
Very long shot			
MUSIC			
SOUND EFFECTS			
DIALOGUE			
DESCRIPTION OF MOVEMENTS	At fade-in: Stationary camera takes detailed eye-level shot of billboard picture of Susan Alexander.	Camera cranes up for detailed shot of sign (1) on top of bldg., with skylight (2) in background (i.e., in long shot).	Camera dollies in for detailed shot of skylight and tilts down for high-angle view of tables and of Susan in background, then starts to dissolve in until a dissolve to:

Fig. 5. Shot analysis of a sequence from *Citizen Kane* (1941).

	Shot 18		Shot 19	
SHOT NO.	18		19	
LENGTH IN FEET	2,385 m = 7,830 ft.		1,500 m = 4,925 ft.	
CAMERA ANGLE				
FOCAL LENGTH:				
Detail				
Close-up				
Close-middle shot				
Middle shot				
Full shot				
Long shot				
Very long shot				
MUSIC				
SOUND EFFECTS				
DIALOGUE	Susan: Who told you you could sit down? Thompson: I thought maybe we could have a drink together. Susan: Think again. (Awkward pause.) Why don't you people let me alone? I'm minding my own business. You mind yours.		Thompson: John — you just might be able to help me. When she used to talk about Kane — did she ever happen to say anything—about Rosebud? Waiter: As a matter of fact, just the other day — when all that stuff was in the papers, I asked her—she never heard of Rosebud.	
DESCRIPTION OF MOVEMENTS	Camera watching Susan in long shot from high angle.	An eye-level camera tilts down as Thompson, walking into frame from right, sits at table. Camera dollies in for stationary close-middle shot of Susan and Thompson.	Camera pans to right to follow Thompson to phone booth. CUT.	Cut is to slightly raised middle shot of Thompson making phone call, with camera stationary.
				Camera remains stationary as waiter enters frame from left. The sequence ends in a fade-out.
			Not shown	Not shown
			Not shown	

rial means for presenting plot, character, and thought; his "diction" is likewise pictorial, in spite of words used in the intertitles of silent films or the spoken dialogue of talkies. The source of this diction is reality: whatever motion is capable of being photographed and subjected to manipulation in the cutting room, where strips of film will be cut and spliced, the sounds mixed, and the music adjoined. If successful, the film will have a unity of action, as well as a temporal and spatial order. The effect on the spectator will be the same as that of all art, rightly perceived. His emotions will be engaged by continuity, characterization, thought, and picture, all working together in an aesthetic harmony.

The preceding film analysis (Fig. 5), adapted from a model for students at the Polish State Film School, provides more articulately and precisely than other written forms the necessary orientation toward communicating what is in a film. It encourages a reader to follow continuity visually and aurally without reducing a complex narrative method to a simple plot summary, or a coherent succession of shots to a set of descriptive words and dialogue. The film again is *Citizen Kane*.

After the prologue, which is set in the projection room where newspapermen watch the "News on the March" documentary of Kane's career, the reporter named Thompson begins his quest for the meaning of Kane's last utterance, "Rosebud." This is the beginning of the story proper.

In the sequence that follows, Thompson goes to Atlantic City to interview Kane's former wife, Susan Alexander, now an aging, whiskey-voiced night club singer. As shot 17 opens we see first a rain-drenched billboard displaying Susan's picture, then a garish electric sign on a squalid rooftop advertising her performance. A skylight is seen in the distance, and the camera moves in closer in order to look down through it. We see Susan sitting at a table in a drunken stupor.

In the next shot (18) the camera seems to have moved through the skylight to get closer to Susan just as Thompson, uninvited, joins her at the table and tries to get her to talk.

In the last shot (19) Thompson, rebuffed by Susan, makes a phone call to his editor from a booth in the club, and after hanging up asks the waiter if he ever heard Susan mention "Rosebud."

As the detailed analysis of this sequence on the accompanying chart shows, the cinematic method of storytelling is both complex and dynamic, involving—in addition to dialogue and sound effects—various camera movements and angles, different directions of movement for camera and actors, and a variety of devices for linking shots. The legend reveals how through the duration of a shot (represented in feet) the camera may be stationary (⊢–––––⊣); panning (∿); tilting up (⌃⌃) or down (⌄⌄); craning up (⌃⌃) or down (⌄⌄); traveling (•——▸); or dollying in (⊥) or out (⊤).* It may be placed at a high angle (⌇) or low angle (⌇) or merely at eye level (▭). Actors may of course also be moving in various directions, as the different arrangements of dotted lines (– – – – – –) in the legend and on the chart indicate.

Some of the ways in which shots are joined together to maintain the continuity of action are also shown in the sequence under analysis. The first shot (17) is joined to the prologue with a fade-out (∇) / fade-in (∆) to make us feel that a considerable amount of time has passed. The shot ends with a dissolve (✗) not only in order to get the camera inside the skylight but probably to make it seem as if the camera eye itself, intent upon its search for the truth, can easily go through glass. The next shot (18), in which Thompson tries to interview Susan, ends with a cut (⊹) to Thompson at the phone booth. Finally, the last shot in the sequence (19), in which Thompson phones his editor and tries to extract further information from the waiter, fades out.

Very little of the film's "plot line" is developed in the three shots diagramed. In fact, both the identity of Susan and the futility of Thompson's mission are completely revealed in the dialogue occupying only a part of the second shot. But the continuity of dynamic visual compositions which Welles builds up through camera placements and movements, and through the careful juxtaposition of shots, cinematically adds much more to the story. When, for example, the camera cranes upward from Susan's billboard portrait to the depressing neon sign and rain-drenched rooftop, Welles lends an intentional irony to what appears at first to be a "rise to the top" motif. And by making us view Susan through the skylight from a high-angle placement of the camera, he forces us to look at the character condescendingly. Thus by advancing his story in this complex visual way, Welles has added to it another crucial dimension: a tone or a point of view.

---

* In traveling, trucking, or dollying (all synonymous terms) the camera moves as an entire unit, often "tracking," i.e., following, an object. When it dollies in or out, it moves either directly toward or directly away from the object. In a crane shot the camera is on a crane, or boom, that enables it to move in or out, but principally up or down, over great distances. In swish-panning the camera swings on its vertical axis at such a fast rate that the scene being photographed is momentarily blurred.

CHAPTER THREE

Visual Rhythm Within the Shot

THE moviegoer who has been following a film story, who is aware of
the contribution of setting and scenery, who is absorbed with the actor's
impersonation, and who even appreciates the values of the camera work,
still falls short of the full experience of film. There is in each movie
an overriding pictorial design and a means through which it is achieved,
and to recognize these is to know the satisfaction of perceiving the
presence of a single mind imposing a special and even unique form
upon the material. This ordering mind, this unseen force, is that of the
director or film editor who leads the moviegoer which way he will. He
orders and juxtaposes each shot, he sets the pace by determining the
length of shot duration through cutting. In short, he arranges all the
fragments, all the elements of the film.

The *cinéaste*—as the French call the moviemaker—is comparable
to a sculptor, a painter, a composer, or a poet. He sets the terms for his
material and accommodates it to his medium. The resultant film that is
his work derives from his vision as an artist. In James Joyce's *Portrait
of the Artist as a Young Man*, Stephen Daedalus says that the artist,
"like the God of creation, remains within or behind or beyond or above
his handiwork, invisible."[1] The history of film offers a grand catalogue
of such artists: Méliès, Porter, Ince, Griffith, Chaplin, Dreyer, Stroheim, Pabst, Murnau, Eisenstein, Lubitsch, Sternberg, Clair, Ophuls,
Renoir, Hawks, Ford, Kurosawa, Bergman, Hitchcock, Fellini, Antonioni, Resnais, Rossellini, Godard, and many others. All these directors
excel, among other things, in being able to create a pattern of visual
rhythm in their work.

Rhythm always provides regularities within a larger movement.

It is a source of aesthetic pleasure that the film shares with and some-times even derives from other plastic arts and from literature. Let us say that we are viewing a painting or a photograph of a nude sitting in a chair. We see the two objects—the person and the chair—not only separately but also as an integrated whole. That is, the contour of the back of the chair may be followed with the eye so that its line may be observed to flow directly into the contour of the nude's thigh. The figure and the chair are thus connected by a structural line fixed in time and space.

In order to observe a piece of sculpture completely, it is necessary to move about it or to have it revolve on its pedestal. As the movement takes place, the structural lines of the statue appear to be altered in relation to one another from moment to moment and give the effect of fluid movement.

In the performing arts, such as theater and dancing, the movement becomes organic as the actors and dancers constantly alter the structural lines of their position. As their position on the stage changes, their relation to the background changes, or the background itself may move, as in a moving cyclorama. While in viewing a statue the spectator may move, generally in the theater he may not.

When one examines a still photograph, one is watching fixed structural lines. When this picture is a frame in a movie being pro-jected, the structural lines shift into rhythmical patterns that create tempo.

The freedom of film allows all three bases of motion: the object viewed, the background, and the spectator. The moviegoer, of course, remains fixed in his seat, just as does the theatergoer, but the camera, which guides his way of seeing the material, is moving: it focuses, it frames, it pans, it tracks and so on, substituting itself for the motion of the spectator. According to Robert Gessner, the theatergoer pays for a fixed view of a stage and sees the play from a close-up, a middle shot, or, if he has paid less for his seat, from a long, high-angle shot.[2] The filmgoer, on the other hand, enjoys variable distances as the camera moves for him.

Movement betokens rhythm, and if we move at a steady pace around a statue, we may notice that, as the lines shift, their regularity sets up visual rhythms that enhance the beauty of the object. Rhythm is particularly appealing to human beings. Life itself, in its essence, is rhythm, as in the beating of the heart or in the cycle of breathing. As Cleanth Brooks and Robert Penn Warren point out, "We know how the moans of a person in great grief or pain tend to assume a mechanical pattern."[3] The very universe, from the phases of the moon to the opening and closing of a flower, reveals an infinitude of rhythms.

The camera is particularly capable of reproducing the universal motions of life. In fact, Gessner defines cinema as "the creation of rhythms amid illuminated objects and to accompanying sounds to express meaning and emotion."[4] The filmgoer who fails to recognize the visual rhythm at work in a great film is therefore deprived of one of the fundamental elements of film enjoyment.

Any artistic structure is an area in which rhythms are worked into a harmonious pattern; one speaks of the "structure" of a poem, a painting, a piece of music, or a novel. Upon rereading Dreiser's novel *An American Tragedy*, Irving Howe discovered what he called its narrative rhythms in the form of "a series of waves, each surging forward to a peak of tension and then receding into quietness, and each, after the first one, re-enacting in a more complex and perilous fashion the material of its predecessor."[5] He also called attention to the repetition of physical forms, such as the rowboat, as well as of scenes, events, and feelings, thus reading Dreiser cinematically.*

If a filmgoer is alert almost exclusively to a film's narrative elements to the neglect of its visual rhythms, he hinders his enjoyment. Alfred Hitchcock's *Marnie* (1964) is a good example. The story lacks distinction, being merely another psychological melodrama with stock Freudian situations. The narrative rhythms, unlike those in *An American Tragedy*, lack such subtlety of experience as we find in life. However, the visual rhythm displays such excellence that Andrew Sarris is able to call *Marnie* "an *ambitious* failure."[6]

The story involves a beautiful woman, Marnie, who burglarizes the firm for which she works, remaining both criminal and sexually unfulfilled, even after marriage to a rich man. The plot is a working-out of her neurosis. The cause of her criminality is shown through a traumatic childhood scene in which she assists in the murder of a sailor her prostitute mother has brought to the apartment. This establishment of a child motif enables the director to develop a rhythm of mounting suspense and anticipation through the repeated appearances of children,

---

* Narrative rhythm is reinforced, Howe adds in the same article, by "Dreiser's frequent shifting of the distance he keeps from his characters," so that at times we feel "locked into the circle of Clyde's moods" and at other times, when Dreiser pulls back, "the sense that Clyde is but another helpless creature among thousands of helpless creatures struggling to get through their time." Thus closeness and distance alternate in a rhythmic pattern. Of course, narratives, since they use language, also include the rhythm inherent in words.

particularly in the form of a blond girl. When, early in the film, Marnie visits her mother, she envies a neighbor's fair-haired little girl because of the affection her mother lavishes on her. Later, in a restaurant, as Marnie converses with her unsatisfied husband, we see gradually re-

Courtesy of Universal Pictures

Fig. 6. *Marnie* (1964). The open purse as a Freudian symbol.

vealed in a booth behind Marnie a blond child sitting with her mother. At the climax we are shown a flashback of Marnie, herself a blond child, committing a murder. Thus the recurrent form of a light-haired child becomes a visual pattern, an element of the film's visual structure.

Yet Hitchcock is far from content with such a simple pattern, and the form of the child remains but one of many visual patterns that pulsate rhythmically throughout the film. The opening shot, for example, reveals a yellow purse, folded in two so that it resembles a vagina. This is continued as a rhythmically repetitive form in objects which, like a purse, are generally thought of as Freudian female symbols (Fig. 6). Since Marnie's preoccupation with opening drawers, safes, and doors shows her subconscious desire to be freed of sexual inhibitions, Hitchcock fills the screen with such objects opening and closing. In an elaborate pattern that pervades the film, he has Marnie in a constant state of awareness of whether doors are open or closed to her. Her subconscious fixation leads to burglary, for she feels compelled to open drawers and safes (Fig. 7). Thus sequences involving

Courtesy of Universal Pictures

Fig. 7. *Marnie* (1964). The open safe and Marnie's guarded liberation.

the blond child are reinforced by shots of objects that represent a secret meaning. The last scene of the film shows a crowd of children in front of the mother's house, as in an earlier visit, taunting Marnie with a sinisterly childish song:

> Send for the doctor,
> Send for the nurse,
> Send for the lady
> With the alligator purse.

The first picture in the film is that of a purse and the last word is "purse," a subtle linking of image and sound.

Other rhythmical effects involve flashes of lightning, the colors red and white, and a tapping noise—all of which come together to create a visual and thematic climax. Whenever Marnie becomes aware of the color red, Hitchcock daubs a part of the screen with this color, to show that the thought of red obsesses her. The whiteness of lightning suffuses her during a thunderstorm but also indicates her fear of white and of lightning. At a race track she becomes entranced by the red-and-white colors of a jockey's uniform. A tapping noise also occurs, providing a clue to the husband-hero about his wife's psyche: "You Freud. Me Jane," says Marnie during a coy dialogue at her husband's attempted psychoanalysis. After a series of cross-cuts from present to past, the final sequence brings lightning, color, and noise into flowering: one stormy night a tapping noise awakens the child Marnie when her prostitute-mother brings home a sailor, in white uniform; after the sailor's death, his T-shirt reddens (reminiscent of the previous flashes of red).

Obviously these pictorial details have symbolic value which the moviegoer addicted to the narrative element will perceive, but unless he is cinematically oriented, he is likely to derogate the film's visual merit. As symbols that are a part of the narrative rhythm, the details noted above seem to be mere commonplaces of the psychological story. But if the filmgoer is alert to the rhythm of shots and has followed the visual details—the blond child, the purse, the door, red, lightning, and the sounds of thunder and tapping—in order to perceive the pattern of picture and repetition of forms, he will find much that is fascinating. As Gessner puts it, "the drama- or literary-minded filmgoer is prone to recall scenes while the . . . cinematically orientated filmgoer refers pragmatically to shots. . . . The cinema-minded is shot-conscious."[7] It is the *shot*—the basic unit of film making—which sets up the kinds of visual rhythms we have been discussing.

According to standard dictionaries, a shot is "a photographic record; a single photograph, or a sequence in motion picture film."[8] In cinema the single photograph is known as the *frame*, or the *still*.*

* Eisenstein equates the single frame with the shot, calling the shot so understood the "minimum 'distortable' fragment of nature." Thus shot is comparable to the color red, which by the addition of blue can be made into violet; or the sound of a note, which by additions of other sounds may be made into a chord. Eisenstein, therefore, means by "distortable" the capacity of a "shot" to be combined with other elements, visual or aural, and made into a montage phrase.

Montage is the combination of two or more distortable units to produce a third

The series in motion picture film is called the *shot*. Spottiswoode defines *shot* as "a segment of film within which spatial and temporal continuity is preserved."[9] Gessner simplifies the definition as "one camera operation."[10] When a scene is being photographed, a shot is what happens between the time the director says "Action" or "Roll 'em" until he yells "Cut." Or, when the film is being assembled in the cutting room, it is the strip of consecutive frames of action that the editor finally chooses to splice into the total film. A shot, therefore, is a basic unit of film, as the basic unit of prose is the sentence, or of a dance, the step, the unit that records motion taking place over a period of time across a certain space.

In art, rhythm requires a pattern in which there is repetition of beat, object, or forms. In a film it may be achieved within the shot when the character or objects move, the background moves, or the camera moves—or perhaps a combination of these. The first movements in cinema corresponded to those in the theater: either persons or objects moved, the camera remained fixed, and the background behind the main figures moved or was stationary according to circumstance. One of the earliest films, Edison's *The Kiss* (1896), consists of only one shot, i.e., one camera operation. The camera remains fixed and there is no background movement. The performers, a man and a woman, face each other and kiss. In Andy Warhol's *Kiss* (1964), the same subject is revived as in each of several shots the camera discovers women kissing different men. Similarly, Warhol fixes on a single area in *Eat, Sleep, Empire,* and *Haircut* (all made in 1964). Together with his *Kiss*, these films seem to return to the primitive cinema technique of the nineties, when the sight of a train pulling into a station or of waves breaking against a beach enthralled nickelodeon audiences. These "primitives" provide simple rhythms. A skillful director like Eisenstein is able to make such movements in front of a stationary camera more artful by the choreographic arrangements of the objects themselves. The procession coming to recall Czar Ivan back to St. Petersburg in *Ivan the Terrible,* Part I (1945), is a striking example, Ivan in the

---

unit independent of the two elements that form it. Thus in an example from Chinese ideograms a dog plus a mouth equals "to bark." And in an example from film, a shot list, say, of a bush in bloom, of the bush losing its leaves, and of the bush covered with snow, we have "three details of a material kind [that] yield a perfectly finished representation of another kind—psychological." One difficulty with Eisenstein's terminology lies in the fact that the shot sometimes refers to a single frame and sometimes to *shot* as conventionally understood, that is, to a series of frames that depict the same scene, setting, or reality. See *Film Form,* edited by Jay Leyda (New York: Meridian Books, 1957), pp. 5, 32, 37, 236-37.

foreground providing the "fixed measure" as the crowd passes him in a curved line.

Porter's *The Great Train Robbery* contains a shot in which background motion is the primary rhythm. As the camera fixes upon the interior of a railroad station house where a gunman holds the clerks at gunpoint, the viewer's attention is directed through a window to the background of this scene in which the train to be robbed slowly comes into the station.

Also vitally important to visual rhythm is the moving camera. The simplest and most common example of the camera in motion as the only variable is the opening shot in westerns in which the camera pans over motionless mountains and plains, or, in the first few moments of films that take place in a large city, when the camera shows aerial views of huge buildings and skyscrapers. It is highly dramatic when Griffith pans the carnage of a Civil War battlefield. Such shots become rhythmically important when the camera movement not only portrays setting but also shows a conjunction of two forms, as seen in the following sequence from John Ford's *She Wore a Yellow Ribbon* (1949):

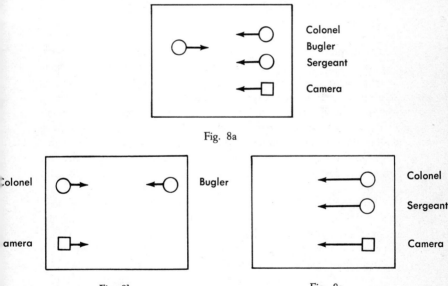

Fig. 8a

Fig. 8b

Fig. 8c

Fig. 8. From John Ford's *She Wore a Yellow Ribbon* (1949).

The colonel (John Wayne) and his sergeant (Victor McLaglen) leave a tent and walk to the left, as the camera follows (Fig. 8a). It would be meaningless movement if they walked for no reason, and therefore Ford places a bugler, facing right, before whom the colonel stops and to whom he gives orders; the camera, having found its destination, also comes to rest (Fig. 8b). A later shot, in which the colonel leaves a cemetery, also joins two forms: in this movement the colonel walks to the right with the camera tracking him, until he stops before the form of the bugler, now at the right (Fig. 8c).

In both these shots, a moving character and a tracking camera lead to the same point of rest, the bugler. Two shots at different moments display a harmonious balance of motion and rest that is part of a well-made film. Furthermore, the parallelism of movement serves to bind the two scenes, like a refrain in a ballad.

The addition of background movement to that of character and camera may make the pattern even more complex, and yet harmonious. In the final sequence of 8½ (1963), Fellini uses all three types to provide a pageant of motion. As Guido moves from left to right with the camera tracking him, he meets all the people of his past life moving in procession from right to left. Thus the left-to-right movement of both the principal figure (Guido) and of the camera is met—almost challenged—by the right-to-left movement of the figures in procession. When the procession forms into a dancing circle moving counterclockwise, the contrasting rhythms of movement become more complicated, but still coordinated, because the foreground figures are now moving from right to left as the background figures are completing the circle by a left-to-right direction. When Guido joins the dancers, a harmonious feeling is rhythmically enhanced by the subjugation of Guido's individual lateral movement to the massive and overwhelming circular one: thematically, the sequence shows that Guido has come to terms with those forces of his past who are dancing about him and with whom he conjoins (Fig. 9).

Still another means of achieving rhythm within a shot is the placement of the camera on a dolly (a flat movable platform) or on a boom (atop a crane) and moving it toward or away from its object. When in Fleming's *Gone with the Wind* (1939) Melanie, part of a group of Southerners shown in middle shot, learns that the Civil War has started, the camera dollies in with stately persistence, moving from a medium shot to a close-up of her troubled face. Conversely, in Milestone's *Of Mice and Men* (1939), after an intimate "two-shot"—a close-up of George (Bur-

Fig. 9. 8½ (1963). A visual reconciliation of Guido and his past.

gess Meredith) and a foreman (Charles Bickford) shown in profile—
the camera moves back on the boom in a diagonal sweep. As the two
men separate from each other, still kept in two-shot, the camera eye
moves from close-up, past middle shot, to the long shot of the great barn
interior in which the men have been sitting.

Tracking movements, in which the camera on a boom, a trolley, an
automobile, or a helicopter follows a moving form, supply rhythm to a
shot. In following the course of a runner or a moving object, be it over
rooftops in thrillers or across prairies in westerns, the camera periodically
reveals similar forms, masses, or light values, sometimes behind, sometimes part of, the moving figure. A kind of visual rhythm, or beat, however irregular, is established.

For particular rhythmic effects within the shot, the film artist employs camera techniques that distort motion, sometimes speeding up or
slowing down the natural rhythms within a shot to convey dream states
of nonrealistic atmosphere.* Speeded-up action is used in *Tom Jones*
(1963) when Tom in his nightshirt runs from the "husband" of the
woman with whom he is about to sleep. A teen-ager's New York is
evoked in George Roy Hill's *The World of Henry Orient* (1963) by
slow-motion effects: one girl leaping over a hydrant descends so slowly
that she appears to defy the laws of gravity; the slow tempo makes the
girl move across New York in an unnaturally slow way that emphasizes
the grace of her actions as well as the easy way in which she encounters
objects. The same effect in Richard Lester's *A Hard Day's Night* (1964)
reveals the Beatles playfully leaping into the air and descending as if
with parachutes. In Andrew Meyer's experimental film *White Trash*
(1965), a satire on white attitudes toward Negroes, slow motion is used
for great satiric effect. When he shows a Negro worker moving an object
from one place to another, Meyer slows the movement in order to ac-

---

* Filmgoers are sometimes puzzled about why physical movements in old-time
movies seem jerky. In early 35 mm films the camera operated at 60 feet of film per
minute, but a realistic sense of movement requires that more than 60, or as many as 90,
feet per minute be projected. Some modern projectors contain a compromise switch
which allows an increase of the rate at which silent film passes through the projection
gate, increasing the number of frames to more than the usual 60 feet per minute for
silent speed but less than the average 90 feet for sound speed. Even when run at this
rate, an old film may still show jerky movement because during splices of broken film
one or two frames of an action—part of the footage—are simply lost.

Keystone Kop speeds were, of course, deliberate, achieved by cranking the camera
at a slower rate so that when the film was projected at the usual speed the images
seemed to move faster. In films requiring a sense of slow motion, the camera was
operated at a faster than average speed.

centuate the Stepin Fetchit–like gesture, achieving a routine so comic that the audience laughs at the conventional prejudice about the Negro at work.

Like alterations of rates at which motion is filmed, the use of masking devices within a shot also varies and distorts the natural range of vision, usually for rhythmic emphasis or de-emphasis of particular details. When the iris effect is used, the shutter of the lens is slowly opened (iris-in) or closed (iris-out), revealing or hiding parts of the frame, an effect now achieved chemically in the studio laboratory. Popular during the time of the First World War and the early twenties, this device is occasionally used in modern films by historically oriented directors like Truffaut in *Jules and Jim* (1962), Godard in *Breathless* (1961), and Richardson in *Tom Jones*. Fritz Lang used the iris effect in *Mabuse, der Spieler* (1922) when the protagonist promises that a bomb will go off at a certain time. Lang irises in on Mabuse's watch, and everything else within the shot is masked out. In *The Widow and the Clergyman* (1921), Carl Dreyer continually begins shots by irising in on a significant detail, usually the face of the clergyman, and ends the shot by irising out. The most famous example of the iris-out occurs in *Intolerance* (1916), when the hands of Mae Marsh are encircled by darkness; every other detail is removed from the courtroom scene, so that the writhing hands convey her anguish (Fig. 10).

But as A. R. Fulton points out, even the closing of a door serves as a masking device: "The door opening to reveal Magwitch [in Lean's *Great Expectations,* 1946] is comparable to an iris in."[11] A newspaper over the face of one man in a shot of several men serves to de-emphasize that face by providing a mask for it and directing the viewer's attention to another part of the frame. In *The Man in the Gray Flannel Suit* (1956), as the hero in conversation with a friend during a ride to suburbia on the New York Central complains about his life, the face of a third man, unimportant in the film, who is sitting behind them, is hidden by a newspaper. Thus director Nunnally Johnson conveys the sense of a crowded train and at the same time keeps our attention on the leading character and his friend. The masked-out third man is like an extra syllable in a verse line. In fact, the mask de-emphasizes a particular object within the shot, in order to allow other rhythms within the shot to interplay.

A more recent device that enables the film artist to do what the iris and the dolly shot have done, namely to stress a particular detail

Courtesy of Paul Killiam

Fig. 10. *Intolerance* (1916). The mask of blackness.

within a shot, is the *zoom*, which is achieved by a special lens that enables the film maker to approach a detail within a larger frame, sometimes even in a long shot, and to accent it. The difference between the effect achieved by dollying and by zooming involves three-dimensionality. In dollying, since points in the foreground move in more rapidly than points in the background, a three-dimensional effect is maintained. In zooming, since every point moves in at the same rate, the camera appears to be moving in on a flat surface. Critics who, like Slavko Vorkapich, feel that any loss of three-dimensionality tends toward the anticinematic dislike the zoom and prefer the dolly effect.[12] Bertolucci in *Before the Revolution* (1964) zooms toward and away from the face of the protagonist's sweetheart shown at first in close shot, supplying a regular visual rhythm, like that of a heartbeat. In *Viridiana* (1961), when a group of peasants are dining in a rich man's house that they have overrun, Buñuel begins the scene in long shot, so that the observer can notice thirteen diners in the pose of the *Last Supper*; he then zooms in on the central peasant, who is placed, like Jesus, at the center of the table, but who is eating boorishly. Since Buñuel is deliberately parodying a famous fresco, the zoom effect, which recalls a flat surface like that of the painting, is more suitable (Fig. 11).

Another device that tends to destroy motion, or at least to arrest it,

Courtesy of Audio Film Center

Fig. 11. *Viridiana* (1961). The establishing shot of *The Last Supper*.

is the freeze shot, which, like the zoom, supplies stress. For some moments the screen resembles a painter's canvas or a still photograph. In the *Saga of Gösta Berling* (1924) Mauritz Stiller had the problem of showing the devotion of a young parson at prayer for a long interval. In order to help the actor, who needs to hold himself perfectly still, Stiller merely printed and showed additional identical frames of the parson praying, thus portraying through a freeze the emotion of holiness as conveyed fleetingly by a single pose. In *The Kiss* (1929) Jacques Feyder freezes Garbo's face in a particularly striking profile simply out of devotion to her beauty.

In recent films the zoom and the freeze have been combined as the zoom-freeze, with dramatic effect. In *Fail Safe* (1964) the President agrees to bomb New York because, through a mechanical error, American bombers, unable to be recalled, are about to bomb Moscow. As one bomber approaches New York, Sidney Lumet cuts from it to a sequence of shots showing New Yorkers in various active postures—children roller skating, a man running, a woman hanging out wash. These activities are designed to show normal life and the motions of the living. After the bomb falls, Lumet uses a collection of stills from this sequence: by zooming in on each of the several figures of the stills shown previously in motion, he implies that these New Yorkers die in a single instant. In *The Insect Woman* (1963), a film consisting of widely separated episodes from the life of a Japanese prostitute, the director, Imamura, chooses to end each episode by freezing the protagonist in some trivial activity. Furthermore, he usually captures her in an off-balance position, as, for example, precariously standing on one foot on uneven terrain in order to remove a shoe. Thus both the end of a significant life episode and, as Thomas Hardy would say, the "ongoing of a trivial existence" are conveyed. In the last scene of *The 400 Blows* (1959), Truffaut's delinquent boy, who has been on the run, comes to the sea, which is a dead end for him: Truffaut ends the film by zooming in on the frustrated boy, who faces the audience accusingly, the sea behind him; Truffaut freezes the shot as a kind of intensification. The audience's anticipation that the boy will run into the sea is converted by the freeze into the realization that he will not commit suicide and that he is now without alternatives, unable to live or to die (Fig. 12). The zoom-freeze in this instance is roughly the equivalent of a heavy stress at the conclusion of a piece of music. As a rhythm within a shot, the zoom-freeze startles the viewer by its swiftness in selecting a significant detail, but, like the iris effect or the pan shot, the trucking shot or the dolly shot, its rhythm must be part of a larger sequence and consistent with an established tempo.

In defense of the use of the seemingly anticinematic zoom-freeze, we must argue that movement is meaningful when it alternates with stasis. A good example of this occurs in *The Loneliness of the Long Distance Runner*. When the hero, running, remembers his father's dead face, the camera zooms in on the face the runner is seeing in his mind's eye. The immobile face of the dead father and the "freezing" of camera movement, taken in conjunction with the running boy, create an alternation of movement and stillness, which anticipates the boy's coming to a stop before the finish line at the climax of the film.

Since the movie screen is often like a painter's canvas, the laying

Courtesy of Janus Films

Fig. 12. *The 400 Blows* (1959). The zoom-freeze will stress frustration.

out of multiple images, even when the surface appearance is not three-dimensional, can be artful. Two pleasing examples occur in Ray En-right's *Dames* (1934) and Carol Reed's *Odd Man Out* (1947). During a production number in the former film a prismatic lens is used to multi-ply the image of Ruby Keeler's face to achieve a comic spectacular tone (Fig. 13). In Carol Reed's *Odd Man Out*, the faces of eight separate people encountered during the film by the dying hero appear in the bubbles of beer foam on a table, each lively face having a visual rhythm of its own.

One unusual rhythmical effect within the shot is the dynamic frame, in which the screen itself either seems to enlarge or decrease in size. The simulation of an expanding frame was achieved in silent films, and of a contracting screen in Cinema-Scope (wide-screen projection). By masking the top and bottom of the traditional square screen, the direc-tor of the silent film *Suds* (1920) elongated a shot of Effingham Street with traffic and pedestrians moving along. Gradually the masked areas were filled out with picture, the frame enlarging. A laterally opening iris also gives the sense of enlargement; in fact, it corresponds to the panoramic shot, as when the camera sweeps across a landscape. All such enlargements of a viewing area simulate the pleasure of the searching eye as new objects are discovered by it. Conversely, wide-screen projec-

Courtesy of United Artists Associated

Fig. 13. *Dames* (1934). The joyful rhythm of a multiple image. A musical production number achieved cinematically: "I Only Have Eyes for You."

tion often involves masking side areas as in the icehouse sequence of Kazan's *East of Eden* (1955), where the doorway through which the scene is shot diminishes the playing area; the spectator derives pleasure when the masked areas are filled in in subsequent shots.* Enlargements

---

* The theater has also undergone a similar enlargement of scenic area, a process inherent in reforms initiated in the 1890's. Edward Gordon Craig removed the proscenium arch, which, since it provides a lateral perspective comparable to that of human eyesight, had been thought alone proper for stage presentation. Craig's removal of the proscenium arch made high stage sets possible and conveyed emotional effects like those being achieved by expressionist painters—in spite of the alleged distortion of the normal vision of proscenium theater. (See Janet Leeper, *Edward Gordon Craig*, Harmondsworth, Penguin Books, Ltd., 1948, pp. 8-10). The open, arena staging that has been popular since World War II expands the stage area beyond Craig's limits, and corresponds to 360-degree screens that were used at the New York World's Fair, 1964-65.

and contractions of the viewing area, whether accomplished by the dynamic frame or by masking techniques, can create within a shot a rhythm that underlines basic emotions, such as when a man feels overwhelmed before a sunset or, conversely, shrinks from some nighttime terror.

We have spoken of techniques proved right for the screen, of many variables within the shot and their rhythmical significance in terms of the movements of characters, backgrounds, and camera. Within a shot light and dark can also alternate rhythmically, as when one character—proceeding perhaps from ignorance to knowledge—moves from a dark area of the screen to a lighted one, and another follows the opposite route. Light and dark values not only set a tone (a film maker's attitude) but also provide, often within a single shot, a rhythm. Sometimes within a shot that shows a face in close-up, a director can make the light pass over it from right to left, effecting the variable chiaroscuro that the sun in its periplus makes over an object in nature.

This sunlike movement also works within a whole sequence, particularly in the fade, light increasing during the shot (fade-in) or decreasing (fade-out) at its end. Fulton attributes the discovery of the fade to Georges Méliès:

> It had been Méliès' practice to decrease the aperture of the lens toward the end of each scene to prevent the film's being fogged. When the film was edited, this part was discarded. But one day, by mistake, an uncut film was projected. Méliès noticed that the fading of the scene made a more effective transition—like the slow closing of a theatre curtain at the end of a scene—than an abrupt cut. It was a fade-out, which gave him the idea of a fade-in.[13]

The light values of a shot, or a sequence, that proceed from fade-in to fade-out, provide a startling cinematic effect, whose importance we hope to have conveyed by our comparison with that greatest of all natural rhythms, the rising and the setting of the sun.

CHAPTER FOUR

Structural Rhythm

Each shot, rhythmical and orderly though it be, is merely a tile of a mosaic that is the whole film. Shots are like phrases and clauses out of which the film editor constructs longer sequences which are like "sentences," "paragraphs," and "chapters"; the editor links shots by various devices which are analogous to punctuation. The sharpest transition between two shots—the cut—divides as it joins, as in the *cutaway* to a frightened horse during an outdoor fight sequence in a western. Sometimes the cut serves as an ellipsis within the same scene. A character walking across a room begins his journey; after a *jump-cut* he is suddenly at his destination. Sometimes in the middle of a sequence of shots a director introduces a shot of another character or another setting—an *intercut*—before returning to the first subject. When this device is frequently repeated to form a pattern, it is called a *cross-cut*.

The cross-cut, two or more sequences of story told by intercut, give suspense to the narrative line or lines, as in Griffith's last-minute rescues. In *Intolerance* four narratives—the fall of Babylon, the journey to Calvary, the story of the girl "Brown Eyes" during the St. Bartholomew Massacre of 1572, and the modern story of a young bridegroom about to be hanged for a murder of which he is innocent—draw to a conclusion with four heroic persons in danger. Belshazzar of Babylon dies, Christ is crucified, Brown Eyes is slaughtered—and these three actions occurring in cross-cut set up an anticipation that the framed young man will also be a victim of intolerance. Only his last-minute rescue relieves our fears. (See Fig. 14.) Usually last-minute rescues are too pat, but the one in *Intolerance,* prepared for by no fewer than three disasters, represents the most complex use of the cutaway.

Fig. 14. *Intolerance* (1916). The cross-cut
for suspense in the last-minute rescue:

Courtesy of Paul Killiam

Fig. 14a. To the scaffold.

Courtesy of Paul Killiam

Fig. 14b. The delay in the rescue.

Courtesy of Paul Killiam

Fig. 14c. The hanging foiled.

Another important feature of this technique as applied by Griffith involves the tempo of shots. Griffith progressively shortens the length of each shot as the rescue draws to a conclusion, thereby quickening the tempo and arousing a sense of breathlessness in the spectator. When we thrill to the action during a last-minute rescue in a western, or a cops-and-robbers thriller, or a war film, we are unconsciously responding to such a quickening tempo of the cross-cuts as well as to the story.

Because Kurosawa's *Ikiru* (1960) is an instinct film (expressing the growth of enlightenment) rather than an action film, the tempo of the cross-cuts is stately rather than quick. After a park has been built in a marshy area of Tokyo, mourners at a wake try to determine whether the dead man was responsible for this improvement, as a group of women claim. Kurosawa has each of the guests reveal a detail that, after pictorialization in cross-cut with measured shots of the wake, becomes a piece of the puzzle that in the end proves the dead man actually to have behaved heroically and without betraying to anyone that he was dying of cancer, a fact known to the audience.

A rhythm of cross-cuts need not be steadily accelerated or measured. In *Breathless* (1961) Jean-Luc Godard cross-cuts with a jerky, syncopated speed. In a seduction scene from his *A Woman Is a Woman* (1960), Charles Aznavour sings on the sound track about his lost love and what she has meant to him. Godard shows us Anna Karina's face throughout the song, and intercuts but seldom the face of Jean-Paul Belmondo, by whom she expects to be seduced in order to have a baby. In filming the face of a woman being seduced by means of a song on the juke box, Godard breaks into one mood and jump-cuts into the middle of another. If the sequence showed the undisturbed diapason of the emotions on Anna Karina's face, it would involve a long roll of film. Godard's cutting seems to create a violent rhythm, as opposed to the full-measured visual beat in Griffith's *Broken Blossoms* (1919), where close-ups of Lillian Gish's face show her passing from deep sorrow and apathy to feigned joy, when she forces herself to smile with the help of her fingers.

The cut is a sharp break that allows the rhythms of the shots it divides to interplay. As we have said, the rhythm of juxtaposition creates a visual equivalent of poetic meter. The length of shot duration—"normally" from four to forty seconds—is analogous to meter in verse, or to tempo. In *Low Country* (1953) a man and a woman are sitting in a moving stagecoach. Shot No. 1 shows both of them for five seconds (an establishing two-shot); shot No. 2 shows the woman and the prairie in the background for ten seconds; shot No. 3 cuts to the man and the country behind him and lasts for ten seconds; shot No. 4 returns to shot 1 and lasts five seconds. The visual form corresponds to the metrical form of an *abba* stanza—without the rhyme. Thus transitions may lead to a kind of end-stop or run-on verse, the cut and wipe tending toward enjambed verse, the fade and the freeze toward end-stop.

Other linking devices are themselves rhythmic, like transitional musical phrases that connect two themes or like shaded areas of blue-green between a patch of blue and a patch of green on a painter's canvas, dividing yet subtly blending the two areas. The *dissolve* also artfully blends objects or settings to foster a sense of the mystery of life. In transformation scenes, as when a childhood shot ends and a manhood shot begins, a story element can be artfully portrayed through the simple dissolve of the face of the boy into that of the man. If the man then passes into old age and if a similar dissolve shows this transition, the linking device serves the film as a form of visual rhyme. The *iris* also serves to link two shots and to achieve the effects of cinematic rhyme. For example, as one shot is ending in an iris, a face may remain framed by the lens (and the iris), but the iris may not be completed; the lens then opens onto the same face in a new setting.

The *wipe* also provides a link between two shots, both of which share the screen momentarily (see Fig. 15). A second image "wipes" (compare the action of a windshield wiper) a first from the screen and may do so in several directional and formal ways: horizontally (1 and 2), vertically (3 and 4), diagonally (5 through 8), in the shape of a fan (e.g., 57 through 76), like the movement of the hands of a clock (79, 81, 84, 85), with a "flip" (the frame revolves 360 degrees), and with continual iris-in and iris-out motion (e.g., 29, 30). The iris and the *explosive wipe* (120) are also a form of masking. A half-wipe becomes a split screen. In *Indiscreet* (1958) Stanley Donen splits the screen with a vertical line to allow Cary Grant, lying in bed, and Ingrid Bergman, in her bed in another part of London—in a telephone conversation—to seem to be occupying the same bed and moving toward each other as if to make love. At the end of the shot, the wipe, which one anticipates will conclude by moving right, instead recedes to the left, from where it came, before the shot fades out.

Another way of linking shots was discovered by accident by Georges Méliès. While filming traffic in Paris, he discovered that his camera had jammed. After adjusting it, he began to film the same area once again. When he later ran the film, "he was startled to notice that an

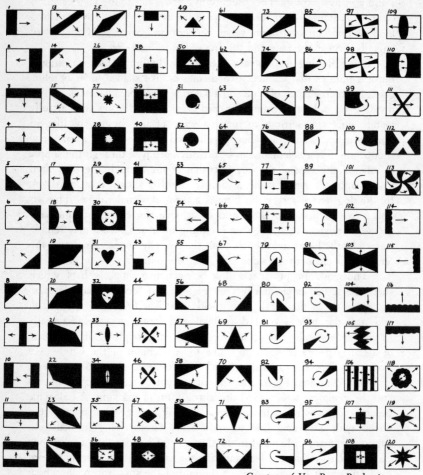

Courtesy of Van Praag Productions

Fig. 15. Wipe chart.

omnibus suddenly changed into a hearse and men into women."[1] This effect of *stop photography* enables two camera operations to film the same scene, in reality two shots appearing as a continuous single shot—a trick useful for conveying supernatural effects or for showing transformation scenes in which objects change their appearance before the eyes of the spectator.

Interpolated shots are an easy means of linking events into a uniform chain. By showing a parade of marching men, the activities before the big game, streamers and tin horns at a New Year's Eve party, and wiping and dissolving these brief shots quickly, the film maker is able to join groups of rhythmically balanced scenes and to present visually the passage of time. Another link to show the steady beat of the the passage of time involves superimposition: a clock's hands move or calendar pages are torn off, while another image, such as that of a man working in prison, accompanies it.

A new genre of film, in which the rhythm of shot linkage, as well as the tempo within the structure of shots, is made of paramount importance, is now being introduced more and more into screenings of experimental films. The "loop film," as the genre is called, consists of a short strip of film which has its ends spliced together into a loop so that it runs through the projector over and over again (without rewinding) and which contains two or more shots or some variation in the composition of the film.

George Landow's "loop film" entitled *Film in Which There Appear Edge Lettering, Sprocket Holes, Etc.* (formerly called *This Film Will Be Interrupted After Eleven Minutes for a Commercial*) is an example of how structural rhythms generated within and between shots can evoke a predominating feeling of rhythmical movement. It consists of a segment of black leader (an opaque strip of film preceding the opening shot) followed by an image, in middle close-up and in color, of a beautiful girl blinking her eyes once. The "take" was made on 8 mm stock but printed on 16 mm so that several contiguous frames, together with the sprocket holes, marginal footage numbers, and frame lines of the original strip are visible. Moreover, a variation in the shot is produced by splicing the exposed material to the black leader in such a way that in the first few seconds the image flutters in the projection gate and goes out of focus. Thus the continual repetition of the pattern of black, flutter, and image-seen-in-frame emphasizes an over-all movement in tempo. Furthermore, the sight of the moving sprocket holes and marginal numbers on the printed filmstrip draws our attention away from the image merely as image, despite its richness of color and intrinsic beauty, and forces us to concentrate on the mechanical movement of the film through the projector even within the shot itself. At the same time the eye blink adds a further beat to this internal shot movement, which in turn forms a measure within the larger tempo of the loop.

As we can see, the subject matter of the "loop film" is made almost completely subordinate to the kinesthetic sensation derived from successive repetitions of the film's parts and to a rhythmical awareness of how the film structure is put together.

We have already pointed out that cinematic movement may mean that the object moves, the background moves, or the camera moves, or any combination of these three. Furthermore, the nature of a movement requires that it continue for a given time in a given direction, and within a single shot the direction of movement across the frame can be prolonged by having the camera track the moving object or pan and tilt with it. However, it would seem to be the tendency of a cut, which ends one shot and begins another, to terminate a given movement abruptly. But this need not be the case, for, quite the contrary, the cut —one of the most creative, although most unobtrusive, devices of film making—can be used to enhance rather than obstruct a directional flow of movement.

An imaginative director or film editor need not accept a cut as a chaotic disruption or dislocation of a line of movement in a sequence of shots. Just as it is possible to bind two or more shots into a rhythmic pattern by continuing a form, color, or texture from one shot to the next, so also is it possible to reinforce the structure of a film by carrying a type of movement through a series of shots ending in cuts. The so-called jump-cut is the most obvious example: a long shot of a cowboy beginning to walk across a corral (from left to right) toward his horse —then a jump-cut to a middle shot of the man (still walking to the right) arriving at his horse.

In jump-cutting, the scene and subject, as well as the direction of movement, are the same. When shots of different objects and locales are juxtaposed, a similarity of directional movement may be a key factor in relating them to a continuous "melodic line." A director maintains a single direction of movement in the following series of five shots: (1) a man runs from left to right; (2) a train moves from left to right; (3) the man runs alongside the train, both passing across the screen from left to right; (4) a dog, sensing that his master is leaving, runs along a road in the same direction; (5) the man jumps aboard the train as the left-to-right movement continues. Of course, in this instance there is the further harmony of image repetition (the separate images of man and train are gathered together and repeated in shots 3 and 5), and the placing of the shots is also guided by the requirements of plot coherence.

Reversal of the directional line in one shot in the series would create conflict and disharmony. But sometimes such a disruption, like a planned discordant note in music, really serves some larger concept of harmony. For instance, in the example just used, if it were necessary to interpose, between shots 4 and 5, a shot of the villain driving his car to the railroad station to intercept the running man, the director might show the car moving in the opposite direction, from right to left, in order to stress dramatic conflict. In Antonioni's *La Notte* the various objects used as projectiles (such as a low-flying jet, flailing fists, rockets, a woman's compact) startle the spectator by being propelled in unexpected directions. (See Chapter Five, pages 93–94.) Here the breaking up of the directional line of movement serves to suggest the spontaneous vitality which the couple lack in their diurnal round of predictable activities.

From the very beginning, following a map analogy, film makers established the convention that right-to-left movement across the screen in outdoor scenes indicated travel from east to west. The journey of pioneers to California—a standard opening scene in westerns—is most often represented by right-to-left movement. In Georges Méliès' *Le Tunnel sous la Manche* (1907), the implicit map analogy gives dramatic coherence to the directional lines in the film (Fig. 16). Two men dream of a tunnel being constructed under the English Channel, and during the photographed vision of the engineering operations we automatically assume that the group of diggers on the right (east) are French and those on the left (west) are English. When Méliès cuts to a full shot of only one group of men digging, we know they are French because the tunnel opening is at the right. Later when he shows us a train about to leave a station and facing left we realize that this too is French. At this point Méliès introduces some suspense by intercutting with shots of a train which we know to be English because it is pointing to the right and which we therefore expect to collide with the French train in the tunnel—a fear soon realized.

A more complex use of directional cutting in accordance with a map analogy is found in Victor Seastrom's *The Wind* (1928). From the opening shot, when a train passes from right to left across the

Fig. 16. *Le Tunnel sous la Manche* (1907).
Directional lines according to a map analogy.

Courtesy of the Museum of Modern Art

Fig. 16a. Digging from France to England: from right to left, east to west.

Fig. 16b. Digging from England to France: from left to right, west to east.

Courtesy of the Museum of Modern Art

screen, the movement from the East of the United States to the West is established. When, after a dissolve, Lillian Gish appears in the interior of the train, the background behind her shows the western countryside passing in the direction suitable for the passage from east to west. Seated backwards, with her back to the west, and therefore facing the east—the piano music playing "Carry Me Back to Old Virginny"—she does not see the villain, the commercial traveler who will deflower her, approaching her, ogling, from screen right to screen left. He passes her, goes to the water fountain, continuing to eye her, and dashes toward the window she is trying to close because of the strong wind. When the male passengers talk of the wind's fury, a frightened Lillian Gish visualizes the Indian legend of the wind as a white stallion. Since the wind comes from the north according to the legend, the picture she sees emerges at the top of the screen, the equivalent of the north, and, in slow motion, moves toward center screen, dissolving into the frightened face of the girl. Thus two directional movements are presented, that of the left-to-right movement of the landscape to signify the westward movement of the train, and that of a north wind represented by a stallion that appears at the top of the screen and moves toward screen center.

By assuming a map orientation both Méliès and Seastrom had made their directional lines implicitly clear. But since Méliès did his work in a period predating that in which the camera moved, i.e., panned, tracked, varied its distance, etc., he had to make his sense of directional movement in *Le Tunnel* mostly inherent in the arrangement of the objects themselves. It is suggested mainly by the direction in which the men and trains are facing rather than by their motion, for the camera, fixed as it was at a middle distance, restricted the movement of men and trains to only a few feet.

Méliès' success under such primitive conditions illuminates another important point about directional movement—that certain forms and objects, even when kept stationary, may hint at a direction of movement and may be placed into harmony with patterns and lines of actual movement. A symmetrical object like a vase would be quite neutral, but a train, arrow, hand with pointed index finger, or profile of a face would indicate movement by the direction in which it is pointed. In a scene in which two characters are in conversation, the camera might focus first on the right profile of the first speaker, which directs the camera to pan right until it arrives at the profile of the second speaker. If the second person is discovered in left profile (i.e., facing speaker number one), the camera is automatically directed to reverse-pan back to the first speaker. If, however, the face of the second person is discovered in right profile (i.e., he has his back to speaker number one), the camera is given the hint to continue to pan to the right in order to reveal what speaker two (and perhaps also speaker number one) is looking at.

The structural rhythm that is set up by continuing or reversing a line of movement within a shot or over a series of shots ought to be more than a simple matter of harmony. Movement in any direction ought to be toward something significant, and a reversal in direction ought to be motivated by some principle of dramatic conflict (in a story film) or formal contrast (in an abstract film). Within a single shot of *Tom Brown of Culver* (1932) William Wyler creates a character relationship by completing a visual pattern with camera movement. When two boys are sad because the mother of a fellow cadet has died, the camera discovers one boy sitting on his bunk, in right profile, and then pans across the room to the other boy facing him, seen in left profile. The directional line, therefore, unites the two boys who are sharing a sadness about the fate of the third.

Directors who arbitrarily continue or reverse lines of movement, pan or track aimlessly, just to "maintain a certain pace" or keep the screen "busy," use mobile effects for their own sake rather than for their organic contribution to the whole film. In *Normal Love* (1965) Jack Smith is especially prone to the defect of aimless panning: he moves the camera continually to "dead spots" in the thick forest. Contrast Kenneth Anger's more purposeful panning in *Scorpio Rising* (1963). The camera traces the sleek fuselage of the motorcycle in the boy's room and then comes to rest on the boy's boots on the floor, and then, in a later shot, traces the lines of the boy's body to his feet and then to the boots on the floor. By using the camera twice in a similar kind of tracing movement and bringing it to rest in both instances on the boots, Anger stresses the boy's narcissistic identification of the machine with his own body.

The opening sequences of Robert Wise's and Jerome Robbins' *West Side Story* (1961) brilliantly demonstrate the many meaningful ways in which lines of movement may be continued and reversed throughout a series of shots. An early one shows the Jets, a teen-age gang, leaning against a playground fence located at screen right. A stray ball bounces into frame from the left and is caught by one of the Jets, who holds it indecisively, then throws it back to the left. With the fence on the right barring any contemplated left-to-right movement, and the initiation of motion in tossing the ball back to the left

side of the screen, the premise is set up for a series of right-to-left movements of the boys. When one of them remarks, "Man, who says we
got to stay here?" the group moves spiritedly in a kind of dance through
streets and alleys, the camera tracking them through a series of shots
as they go mostly toward the left. In accordance with a map analogy
(the East Side is screen right and the West Side, screen left), they
are, we come to understand, penetrating more deeply into New York's
West Side. In one of the shots of their right-to-left movement the
camera pans rapidly ahead of the group and suddenly freezes upon a
young man who, standing screen left, but facing right, opposes them
with an outstretched arm. It is Bernardo, the leader of the West Side
Puerto Rican "Sharks," and not only does his position act as a barrier
to the Jets' westward movement, but his gesture orders them to retreat
to the East Side. This is reinforced by shots of other members of the
West Side Sharks moving menacingly in this reversed line of direction
in opposition to the Jets, from left to right. When the Jets see they are
outnumbered, they begin running back toward the East Side, continuing the reversed movement indicated by Bernardo. At one point they
are seen passing along a fence on which is chalked a large shark with
gaping jaws. By having the drawing face left so that the Jets seem to
be running directly into the shark's mouth, the director again reverses
the direction of a compositional line and foreshadows the further clash
that will ensue in the gang feud.

Thus it can be seen that every directional line that is continued or
reversed throughout these shots from *West Side Story* has a dramatic
purpose as well as a rhythm that is pleasing. The choreographic nature
of the movements of the actors makes it obvious that this one sequence
is intended as a filmed ballet, but it is the cutting in relation to the
directional lines of movement and composition that makes it a true
ballet of the *cinema*.

Another way in which a film maker may maintain a visual harmony in the structure of his film is by means of the form cut. This consists merely of framing in a successive shot an object which has a shape
or contour similar to an image in the shot immediately preceding, the
two shots together creating a rhythm based on their geometrical con-
gruity and balance. A classic example of this is a sequence in Griffith's
Intolerance in which the camera cuts from the round shield of Belshazzar to the round end of a battering ram as it strikes against the gates of
the city, the circumference of the log striking the screen at precisely
the same points previously traced by the shield. Of course, such effects
usually supplement other kinds of harmony—the logic of plot connec-

tions, the consistency of theme and tone—and are themselves often reinforced by other types of rhythm, like the tempo of shot lengths, musical background, balance of masses, and camera movement. In most of Griffith's form cuts, as in the one just mentioned, the intention is to suggest, by means of identical forms, a similarity of action.

Usually form cuts are not consciously detected as such by the average filmgoer, especially when the shots are juxtapositions of familiar objects customarily found together in the same environment. But such unobtrusive form cutting may nevertheless contribute to the viewer's pleasurable sense of a smooth flow in the film's visual imagery. This is the nature and effect of a scene in Thomas Ince's *The Switchtower* (1915). As the hero is leaving prison, his face is enclosed in the circular frame of an iris. When the frame irises out, it not only reveals the whole man but joins the arch of the prison gate under which he is standing. The formal structure of this visual impression is due to analogies—between the roundness of the face, that of the iris itself, and that of the arch; and the rhythm develops like the widening concentric ripples in a pond. Since the plot had already made it clear that the hero

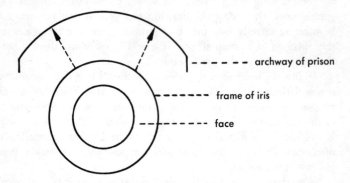

Fig. 17. Thomas Ince's *The Switchtower* (1915).

has served a prison term, the sight of his head under the archway does not strike the audience as unusual, but the arc of the widening iris traveling from head to arch, then beyond, suggests rhythmically, poetically, and thus emotionally, the enlarging sphere of freedom now accessible to the man.*

* Strictly speaking, the iris device is, of course, not a type of cutting, but rather a kind of masking and unmasking. It is, nevertheless, a joining device which, like the cut, connects and reveals the shapes and configurations of objects.

In Emil Holmsen's *Time of Desire* (1953) we find a striking instance in which a form cut is, momentarily, the only means whereby the structural rhythm of the film is sustained. As a young man spies upon two sisters bathing nude in a lake, the camera reveals his staring eyes in close-up. In a subtle cut, or quick dissolve, the eyes transform into billiard balls and the undefined background area into a billiard table. The camera then moves backward into middle shot, revealing a billiard game that actually includes the young man himself. Although the orbital form of the eyeballs is carried directly into the orbital form of the billiard balls, the director's cleverness in finding a formal resemblance between objects not ordinarily associated in nature and not instantaneously useful in furthering the plot seems self-conscious, almost exhibitionistic. The two objects are not made analogous in *function* and *meaning* as well as in form; they are not connected logically, emotionally, or symbolically.

In his famous documentary about the Mississippi River, Pare Lorentz was able to overcome an obstacle inherent in his subject matter largely by means of form cutting. Lorentz has explained that although the Mississippi was intrinsically dramatic as a torrential Minnesota stream, it broadened into long dull stretches as it flowed south of Cairo. Yet his aim in *The River* (1937) was to give a vivid sense of the way in which the waterway gathered in power and importance as it both supported more industries and prepared to wreak the havoc of floods. His chief artistic problem, therefore, was to give the viewer a sense of quickening tempo and of greater momentum as the confluence of other waterways with the Mississippi urged it on to its climactic end.

In large measure this was accomplished by the crescendos of Virgil Thomson's musical accompaniment, by the quickening pace and excitement in the narrator's poetic commentary, and by the metrical arrangement of shot lengths. But if such tactics were not to seem a false and melodramatic heightening of emotion, they had to be verified by the photographic image itself. Lorentz' solution was to cut continually from the dull placid river to more "dynamic" objects associated with it—objects which either by their circular motion or their circular form suggested the "rolling" quality of the river. Thus he cut to the turning gears of the locomotives and machines operating as part of the river's industry, and highlighted the dramatic billows of steam emanating from them. The formal rhythm of this latter image was sustained by cutting to shots in which the river was overhung with large billowing clouds. When these shots were further intercut with such scenes

Fig. 18a

Fig. 18b

Fig. 18c

Courtesy of Pare Lorentz Associates, Inc.

Fig. 18. *The River* (1937). Form cutting to show dynamic movement. Clouds (Fig. 18a), bales of cotton (Fig. 18b), and eroded land masses (Fig. 18c) as corresponding forms and textures of the Mississippi River.

as logs spinning into the waterway, the smooth slopes of land eroded by the river, and the bales of cotton rolled along the wharves by Negroes as the narrator chanted:

> We rolled a million bales down the river for Liverpool and Leeds;
>   1860: we rolled four million bales down the river;
> Rolled them off Alabama,
> Rolled them off Mississippi,
> Rolled them off Louisiana,
> Rolled them down the river![2]

the audience was given a sense of an undulating rolling force. This effect had been unattainable through the image of the river itself but was easily suggested by intercutting it with curvilinear patterns of objects associated with it or affected by it and more clearly revealing its true essence. (See Fig. 18.)

Form cutting often produces its rhythmical effects in conjunction with other types of reiteration and duplication: that of color, texture, mass, and illumination. The streams and clouds photographed by Lorentz match each other in texture and light as well as in form, and it is in fact chiefly their vaporous, luminous quality which suggests the foaming waters of the river's rapids.

Space play is another concept strongly related to form cutting. It helps to establish an impression of structural unity in object movement throughout a series of shots. To make effective use of "space play," the director first of all establishes certain areas of the screen (or frame) as appropriate to certain objects or characters, and maintains them in these areas from shot to shot.[3] There is, of course, movement of the character or object within its own area. This is similar to an actor in a stage play being free to move but at the same time confined to the range of his own spotlight. Only if the dramatic situation demands it may objects or characters be transposed to different screen areas within a single shot (as in a shot of a violent fist fight between two men), or they may be switched around after a cut (as in a reversed-angle shot of two characters moving toward each other). The effect is somewhat analogous to music in which a dominant key is established within which pleasant variations take place.

Ernst Lubitsch, for instance, was usually careful to identify in early shots the acting areas for his heroes and heroines. In *Bluebeard's Eighth Wife* (1938) the first appearance of Gary Cooper and Claudette Colbert at a department store counter establishes their acting areas: Cooper, screen left; Miss Colbert, screen right. During the succeeding action, especially when the pair appear in a "two-shot," they maintain their screen areas unless the dramatic situation clearly demands otherwise, as for example during a heated argument. Lubitsch, unlike even some of the best directors, never arbitrarily brings his camera across the "stage line" or reverses angles without some aesthetic reason. Rather than make his characters' movements static or theatrical, his adherence to this principle on the contrary allows him the greatest cinematic freedom. He is quite willing to have characters move across the screen or cross it diagonally by gliding up and down stairways, but he handles this variation always with reference to an underlying knowledge of where they belong. Thus the almost subconscious expectation in the audience of where the actors ought to appear from shot to shot becomes one of the dominant keys which rhythmically ties the film together and the variation of which is always pleasing because justified by the exigencies of plot, theme, or character.

Many experimental film makers who avoid story lines and character studies must rely more heavily upon the intercutting of forms, colors, textures, masses, and patterned movements to achieve the continuity of their rhythmic flow and to construct an architectonic pattern for the whole film. In Stan Brakhage's notes entitled, "The Movement of the Animal Form of Cat," written as a blueprint for his film *Nightcats* (1956), we can see that the "meaning" of the cat is that he is both identical with and distinct from the form and substance of his "realm" and that this paradox can be shown cinematically only by the intercutting of harmonious as well as conflicting forms, lines, colors, and light masses:

The black cat, with his various lighted parts, will begin the film— for nightcats will be elicited and evolved rather than shown and told of. The cats will emerge their various colors out of the dark and play their moving parts in relation to the fragments of their realm, the rail, the vegetable growth, and gradually then in interrelation. Perhaps their stage will first be set with the whiting of the rail, the spot of the moon proceeding out of the backdrop of black. . . .

The black cat then begins and, with his eyes, is what he is. And light touches him and his world, withholding only to reveal the more. And he is positioned in the semblance of his world. And he is backed, once fully revealed, by the black which he is part of and which then becomes a part of him. And light may lay a line of himself upon him as illuminated. And the illumination may then move as the line of him. Then the thrust of his legs may chop up the grass of the line and become a grace of its own. And light may play upon the brown of him. And the various lines of him, as illuminated, may reflect his movement. And the brown of him may insist upon attention more than the line.

The black of the cat, and his lines in movement, begin. The browns of him insist on color cat. And the colors evolve in relation to this beginning— thru tonal development and thru contrast—thru linear evolvement and thru linear conflict. . . .

Cat head round as full moon. Cat arched back as curved as quarter moon. Siamese length as horizontal as the rail he proceeds along.

Cat as white as moon as white as rail.

Here we have transitions thru parallel images and colorings.[4]

Such a film makes of the filmgoer the same demand that a painting makes of the sophisticated art connoisseur: an awareness of an object not only as representational but as an extension of the line and color harmony of the whole. To this end, form cutting, regardless of the film's genre, plays a key role in aesthetic appreciation.

We have examined the details that create harmony within the shot and between shots and have shown how directional and formal lines constitute a pictorial harmony. In evaluating the tempo in which the shots are presented, a moviegoer for whom the screen has only the two-dimensionality of a wall will call a movie "slow" when it is actually stately, and filled with lines and forms that merge into intricate patterns, as in a Dreyer or a Satyajit Ray movie or in Eisenstein's *Ivan the Terrible* (1945-46). Nor is a movie fast-moving merely because of fist fights or gunplay, although such action films give the appearance of being fast-paced. James Wong Howe's camera work in the fight sequences of *Body and Soul* (1947) and John Ford's direction of the fist fight in *The Quiet Man* (1952) proceed with visual intricacy and formalism not unlike that of the coronation scene of *Ivan*. *Fast* and *slow* in movies are determined not by the physical speed of human movement but by the pace set in the editing. A director achieves a graceful pace by attention to detail, by holding shots for proper intervals, by making a line of movement lead to a significant detail or to a countermovement. In addition, the balance of accords and oppositions of shots helps determine the proper pacing.

The harmony of pictures may be demonstrated with a shot summary of the opening sections of the first two reels of Hitchcock's *Shadow of a Doubt* (1943). In the first reel, Hitchcock shows a city, Philadelphia, seen from railroad tracks in the outskirts. He cuts to a street of the city, with children playing, and then to an open window of one of the buildings. As he dollies into the window, the spectator sees a man (Joseph

Cotten—"Uncle Charlie") lying fully dressed on a bed. After interior scenes with a landlady, Hitchcock moves Charlie to a window from which he sees two men. When Charlie leaves, these two men follow him. In a poolroom he makes a telephone call, saying, "I want to send a telegram."

Hitchcock then cuts to a new setting, that of a small town. While Cotten's voice is saying, "Santa Rosa, California," the sound montage serves as a link between the two settings. After the establishing shot of the Santa Rosa street Hitchcock cuts (in this second reel) to the window of one of the houses and dollies into the interior where Teresa Wright (Little Charlie) is lying on a bed in much the same posture as Joseph Cotten was. During scenes with her family, who come into her room as the landlady had come into Big Charlie's, Little Charlie reveals that she has been thinking of sending a telegram to Uncle Charlie. When her mother says that Charlie was the youngest in her family, the boy, the youngest "spoiled" son of the Santa Rosa family, is shown.

After Charlie comes to the house, there is much talk of mental telepathy and Teresa Wright says to Joseph Cotten at one point, "I'm glad mother named me after you and that she thinks we're both alike; . . . we are twins." Soon the camera seems to confirm this by showing them even to walk in the same way. But the wonder of this presentation is that Hitchcock has found a set of accords that pictorialize the similarity long before words are spoken. Awareness of these visual harmonies is one of the special joys of going to the *pictures*.

Each cinematic artist brings his visual style to a high point and prepares for further innovations by subsequent artists. The Lumière brothers are justly famous for the stationary camera they set up in order to film real events projected in a fixed frame. Georges Méliès was brilliant in creating trick photography as he arranged vaudeville acts for presentation on a screen. If Edwin C. Porter's contribution was that he was the first to use the camera to film arranged scenes for storytelling, his genius lay simply in seeing that a fixed camera held in medium or long shot could photograph a play. On the other hand, Griffith's genius lay in his recognition that cinema was *not* theater and in his application of devices to establish continuity.

In the work of these early directors, a visual rhythm operated within shots and sometimes in short sequences. Occasional accords between the rhythm of an early sequence and that of a later sequence were theoretically possible, but when they occurred they appeared to be unplanned. The pictures in Eugene Nowland's *Vanity Fair* (1914) rarely have the harmony of directed movement, for the goal was to present multiple settings that tell Thackeray's novelistic story. Another reason for the lack of significant parallels of movement in silent films lies in their abundant use of intertitles. The effect of "titles" on the visual rhythm is such that scenes end quickly; the words interfere with pictorial movement. It is true that Griffith picks up after a title the positions of his performers before the title has been given, but this lapse of time, even when the performer has moved while the audience has been reading, is fatal to the maintenance of plastic movement. Both Griffith and the early Dreyer achieved their poetry through the iris-in and the iris-out that enable concentration on a significant detail of a larger scene, but the dynamic rhythm of movement from beginning to end was not in their art.

Germany's UFA directors, who filmed in studios, tried to do away with titles even before the discovery of sound. Sacrificing captions in order to maintain a fluid visual rhythm from the beginning of a film to its end, F. W. Murnau used street signs or letters of correspondence as integral props, as in *The Last Laugh*, to photograph without interruption for titles.

Lubitsch's genius in shortening time so that an action is presented with intensity and concentration enabled the cinema to proceed by indirection. As Ivor Montague points out,

> The first great innovator of parts of action and time to represent wholes, not merely for speeding the action—a method developed pragmatically and very soon a part and parcel of all skilled cinema technique—but as a witty expression, a sort of visual epigram, was . . . Ernst Lubitsch.[5]

As examples, Montague cites a shot of a hand depositing clothing on a chair as standing for going to bed, a shot of a caller passing through a succession of huge antechamber doors flung open in pairs at his approach as standing for the pomp and power of his host, and a succession of shots of a young lady—a night scene in which she is adamant against the advances of a suitor followed by a morning scene of the lady secretly smiling at a bruise on her white shoulder—as standing for her change of heart.

By the late twenties visual rhythms were extending from the beginning to the end of a film. Cinema is a medium of plastic art, and the problem of what objects and forms were most malleable came to dominate cinema stylists. Chaplin preferred uncluttered screens and placed primary emphasis on details that convey stories—human dramas. After he engaged Joseph von Sternberg to direct *The Woman of the Sea* (called also *The Sea Gull*), Chaplin despised all the shrubbery and columns and confetti that blocked out Sternberg's characters. Both tell stories, but each uses a different visual style. If Chaplin tends toward classical restraint, then Sternberg favors baroque adornment. John Grierson was eyewitness to the conflict between them:

But (I hate to say this) even a masterful intuition cannot take a man everywhere; and Chaplin has his blind spots. It is my guess, for example, that he is . . . blind to the visual beauties of von Sternberg's "The Woman of the Sea." This picture was made for him and Chaplin failed to release it. I think I know the reason because I heard Chaplin go over his own version of "The Woman of the Sea" two nights before von Sternberg showed it to me. Here was Chaplin concentrating on the human drama of the picture—on nothing else; here was von Sternberg concentrating on the visual beauty of the picture—on scarcely anything else.[6]

Whereas Chaplin saw only sweat on the fishermen, he missed, according to John Grierson, "the visual pattern of the rigging, the pattern of sunlight on the drying nets, the statuesque pattern of the human figures."[7]

With the invention of the sound film, the "color" of spoken words was added to that of picture. At first there was some restriction of movement, due to the fixed placement of microphones, but the microphone was soon put on a boom, outside camera range, and directors were free to stress the rhythm of pictures. Ford, Howard Hawks, and Hitchcock continued in the thirties to make movements natural and easy, and they maintained tempos that were pictorially pleasing. In spite of sound, Ford said, "Let the pictures do the talking for you." Hawks used pictorial skills to reinforce his view of the masculinity of men and the femininity of women, telling action stories in which men behave heroically, capturing their heroism in picture, and showing women as exultant in their bodies, as typified in the wiggle of Lauren Bacall's hips as she leaves Martinique in Hawks' version of *To Have and Have Not* (1944). Men and beasts, as well as inanimate objects, are put into a complex rhythmical movement in Hawks' *Hatari* (1961), in which a jeep, a charging rhino, determined agile men, and a moving loop of rope are intercut into an intricate pattern.

Following in von Sternberg's line is the genius Max Ophuls. Penelope Houston writes:

Ophuls's stylistic trademark was the tracking shot: incessantly, flowingly, gracefully, his camera moved across and around the sets on which he expended so much care, from Madame de's dressing-room to the circus-ring of *Lola Montes*. . . . This last film . . . had the scale—the baroque frontage —to support the rococo of its intensely mannered style. . . . Ophuls wanted elegance, and more elegance, and the finest sets and the right to keep that camera endlessly moving.[8]

Orson Welles also is noted for his baroque style, for he loves to fill a shot with detail and to shoot his subject from arch camera angles.

Ford's dictum that pictures should do the talking is essentially true, but it does not acknowledge the rhythms of speech and music that accompany visual rhythms. Sound, whether in the form of dialogue, music, or special effects, ought not be thought of as irrelevant to a director's visual style; rather, it ought to be regarded as a means of enhancing that style. The fact that dialogue has rhythms and speech patterns which may become meaningful adjuncts of visual rhythms is almost too obvious to mention, for the theater from its very inception has used speech poetically to correspond to mood, situation, and pace of action. In films, the slow ruminative speech of a W. C. Fields naturally fits a visual tempo quite different from that which corresponds to the fast patter of a Groucho Marx.

We must point out in this discussion of sounds as adjunctives to visual rhythms a few ways in which speech and dialogue have been used in this regard cinematically rather than theatrically. In *Genevieve* (1954), for instance, a nonsynchronous voice is used as the equivalent of a visual dissolve. As one scene is ending with a married couple about to make love in their hotel room, a voice on the sound track announces, "Ladies and gentlemen, what you are about to witness here has occurred many times before." The audience at first thinks this applies to the couple's love-making, but the delayed cut to a loudspeaker at a fair grounds shows us that it is a commentary on the automobile rally which is about to begin and in which the pair are going to participate.

In *Twice a Man* (1963) Gregory Markopoulos tries to make dialogue correspond to his single-frame editing by electronically interrupting the flow of speech. These staccato passages require the same cultivation of ear in order to be understood as the single-frame projections require a practice of the eye in order to be seen.

Finally, the complete cacophony and incomprehensibility of speech have been used as effectively in films as discords have in music. In Jacques Tati's *Mr. Hulot's Holiday* (1953), the high-pitched sputtering sound of Mr. Hulot's tiny car prefigures the farcical bumbling in his physical movements throughout the film. In the opening shot of the same film, we are shown a loudspeaker on a train platform which is blaring out completely incomprehensible information. This forms a kind of musical accompaniment to the movements of a group of uncomprehending passengers who scurry wildly from one platform to another as trains arrive.

Perhaps an even more valuable adjunct to the rhythm and tempo that spring from the photographic elements of a film is music itself. The movies were never really silent. A piano or orchestral accompaniment was from the first a part of the film experience. When Buster Keaton walked, for example, the sound rhythm of music underlined or underscored the rhythm of his steps. Matching music to the movie effectively is virtually an art in itself. In the poorer-class movie houses of the silent era the piano accompanist was too often an inferior and indifferent musician who either played his "crutch" music without much attention to the mood or type of action on the screen or merely drew upon a stock repertory of old favorites that vaguely corresponded, usually in subject matter rather than in tempo, to the screen action. On the other hand, there were movie-house musicians whose knowledge, sense of "theater," and professionalism enhanced the films they accompanied.

Later, in the thirties and forties, the orchestral accompaniments on sound tracks were sometimes flat, unimaginative, and even incongruous with the mood of the story or the tempo of visual movement. Many Laurel and Hardy comedies of the period have an unvarying "Muzak" type of orchestral score, while Ford's *Tobacco Road* (1941) suffered from the continual monotonous accompaniment of a saccharine violin.

In his book *The Banquet Years*, Roger Shattuck describes in detail Eric Satie's problems in constructing an adequate score for René Clair's *Entr'acte* (1924). The account is particularly illuminating because the film's inclination toward nonsensical dadaism—a sort of "dream without a subject"—rather than toward coherent drama or consistent mood forbade his merely constructing a tone poem or the usual kind of "program music." Shattuck writes:

In 1924 the opportunity arose [for Satie] to write a significant piece of furniture music as background for the film sequence René Clair had made for the Picabia-Satie *Relâche. Entr'acte* or *Cinema*, as the film score was alternately called, conforms absolutely to the contour of Clair's fast-moving montage. The film, a joyous free-hand anticipation of all the nightmare farces the surrealists would later produce, includes as its climactic scene a hearse being hauled around the Eiffel Tower by a camel. The construction of the music could not be more primitive. Satie merely used eight measures, as the unit that most closely matches the average length of a single shot in the film. He fills each of these units with one stereotyped phrase repeated eight times. Between the units he inserts a double line, a new signature, and frequently a change in tempo. The transitions are as abrupt and as arbitrary as the cuts in the film. Typical measures lend themselves to infinite repetition and do not establish any strong tonal feeling.

It makes excellent unassertive film music. Satie counted and timed and trimmed it to fit the movie exactly, and it reinforces the effect of the visual image without ever demanding conscious attention. *Entr'acte*, one of the earliest examples of pure movie music, satisfies the artistic demands of a new medium and the technical demands of live performance. It was a significant step toward finding a satisfactory method of film accompaniment. But removed from its proper context and played alone, the score has no form, no musical identity.[9]

Thus Satie, unlike writers of "crutch" film music whose main problem is timing a mood piece to terminate simultaneously with a scene, invented a kind of "abstract" music based on the correspondence of the structural rhythm to that of the image. In this he anticipated electronic music scores, which, since *Destination Moon* (1950), have been finding their way into films.

Throughout the thirties and forties, Hollywood film makers would shoot the film, make a "rough cut" based on day-by-day *rushes,* and then assign a music editor or a composer to provide a musical score and a sound editor to create proper effects that underscored the visual rhythm. As Elmer Bernstein, a noted film composer, told Stanley Kauffmann, the composer of the sixties works on the film from the beginning. He sees the rushes daily, prepares a main theme, and determines whether the music for a sequence shall be *kinetic,* that is, supplementary to the physical energy of an outdoors film, or *implicit,* a resonance of the action that not only subdivides time with a tick-tock metrical pattern but also concurs with dialogue and picture to convey an emotion that parallels the story. He is aware that music accentuates visual techniques like a cut or a dissolve, and he speaks of framing one sentence of dialogue with music. The role of the music editor is to prepare a post-shooting script that divides the time into the smallest possible units, calibrated from oo units of perhaps 10 seconds or less, and to provide cue sheets that indicate where music is desirable. The composer has to know where silence is effective and where a *tremolo* that stresses what follows will make people nervous. At the final dubbing of sound, when, as Mr. Bernstein says, the dubbing room becomes a nerve-racking place, final decisions determine questions of volume, interference, and silence. In order to keep the music from interfering with dialogue, a quick solution, Mr. Bernstein says, is "woodwind solos above the range of the human voice, kept low in volume." Such a decision often eliminates quarrels about whether the music is too intrusive.

Beyond these uses of music as accompaniment, nonmusical sounds may form auditory counterpoints of visual montage. After early sound films in which the noise of a door closing was simultaneous with the picture of a door closing—a device known as synchronous sound—film makers began to use nonsynchronous sound in which the door closing was not seen, but merely heard, the context providing the meaning of the sound. In other words, a sound image was used in place of a visual image. The combination of synchronous and nonsynchronous sound, therefore, becomes part of the tempo, as in shot 2 of *Low Country* (see pages 58-59), where the dialogue, which is synchronous with the image of lip movements, is blended with the nonsynchronous sounds of the unseen horses's hooves to complicate and complete the visual image.

An impediment to the full enjoyment of cinema lies in the failure of filmgoers to recognize the visual rhythm at work in a great film, howsoever much they may praise it for other elements, such as story, acting, and so on. Using the excuse that they are concerned with the whole film—as all critics must be—or, as Penelope Houston holds, with the humanistic values of a cinematic experience, "popular" critics and unobservant filmgoers ignore the existence of structural rhythms and the visual patterns by which a film proceeds. They are, of course, conscious of beautiful photography and of artful camera angles; they are capable of being dazzled by camera tricks; but they are not aware of simple workmanlike visual patterns that, like poetic meters, sustain a visual progression. The filmgoer must not be involved solely with narrative or with the skill of performer, scriptwriter, or cameraman. To judge properly, he must understand the "rhythms amid illuminated objects" that "express meaning and emotion."[10] Awareness of visual rhythm involves a fuller way of looking at the screen than by passive acceptance of moods and tricks, and supplies a necessary basis for determining the organic nature of cinema art.

CHAPTER FIVE

Imagery

SOMETIMES single cinematic details display great beauty. Garbo's face became so famous a visual image that a critic asked one of her directors, Clarence Brown, what the star was thinking about in those soundless evocative close-ups. "Absolutely nothing," Brown said.[1] Yet the vitality of Garbo's features, like that reproduced in great portraits, seemed to justify the image—Garbo's face enveloped in an appropriate light. Such renditions of life images were sought in still photography by Matthew Brady and in cinema art by D. W. Griffith, who held that an operator must succeed in reproducing in its integral beauty the simple effect of the movement of the wind over water or over the branches and tops of trees, or even more the strong opposition of light and dark on a face. Only then has he succeeded, according to Griffith, in providing what the theater cannot give the spectator.[2] Raw detail and treatment by a great artist lead to artistic realization.

In a poem based on Brueghel's *Fall of Icarus*, W. H. Auden observes that a farmer plowing, a fisherman fishing, a shepherd tending a flock, and a falconer hunting—all these figures turn away from the main figure, the drowning Icarus, who is represented by two pink legs sinking into a blue-green sea. If the farmer, fisherman, shepherd, and falconer are seen as details of the canvas, then they function only as simple *images*. Since each of them, however, is being compared to all the others, each figure functions as metaphor. According to Auden, the old masters understood suffering so that in the main action, Icarus drowning in the sea, "everything turns away from the scene." Each concrete detail—the plowman, the fisherman, etc.—has the same illustrative function; each image is therefore also metaphorical, since it functions in a comparison.

81

Metaphor also establishes an enlarged feeling in a greater context. The first three lines of the following poem are in themselves details, not metaphors, although the fourth line will make them so:

Epigram
I had gone broke and got set to come back
And lost on a hot day and a fast track
On a long shot at long odds, a black mare . . .

These facts about a horse player's day, so long as they are restricted to racing, remain descriptive details, simple *images;* the last line of J. V. Cunningham's poem casts its meaning over them, however, and makes the horse player's actions images of his behavior in life:

By Hatred, out of Envy, by Despair.

The allegory of blood lines so illuminates the preceding details that they display a lifetime's emotions rather than a single day's living. The details now are metaphors, conveying emotion beyond that required for a context of racing.

In modern criticism *imagery* has become a complex word. Any sensuously apprehended detail is an image; hence what one sees or hears in a film is image. In cinema, any sound or picture or part of a picture, since it is representative of something in nature, or in reality, is one kind of image. But an image can also function as an implied or stated comparison, in a context broader than the representational, that is, metaphorically. Finally, like poetry and painting, cinema uses concrete details so that they function as symbols, thought-bearing images that stand for a complex of associations. Symbols, arising when image or metaphor is surrounded by a complex of thought, are a high point of cinema art. On the other hand, as in language, there are in cinema concrete details so conventionalized that they are merely clichés, overused metaphors that no longer convey the beauty they are intended to convey.

Within single shots directors sometimes use an area of the frame, often a window in the background, to create an action that both complements and complicates the main foreground action. A special skill in film making lies in "poetical" use of this area, which we may call the image box. In Edwin Porter's *The Great Train Robbery*, as the robbers enter the station house and hold the clerks at bay, a large window in the station house interior shows the train coming into the station and decelerating to a stop. The men in the foreground remain more or less motionless. Taken together, their virtual immobility and the movement outside the window create suspense, for the train to be robbed must inevitably halt. When a clerk makes an abrupt movement, as if to flee and warn those on the train, and when a robber's gun threatens him, the helplessness of the brave clerk, an emotion that the sympathetic spectator also feels, is reinforced. Since a train moving into a station does not normally contribute to a feeling of helplessness, a commonplace detail has become a metaphor.

In a late shot of *The Best Years of Our Lives* (1946), William Wyler also uses a window as an area of imagery. A demobilized pilot sits at the controls of a bomber that is soon to be junked. Having returned from a glorious captaincy in World War II to poverty and an unfaithful wife, he feels himself to be obsolete and useless. Outside the plane's window, which serves as an image box within the frame, the spectator sees a panorama of junked planes, already seen in a long shot. The panorama reveals the similarity of the unwanted pilot and the doomed machines that were once the source of his glory, so that the foreground and background images complement each other.

A background, vital for maintaining mobility during static scenes, may also be wisely used to convey information unknown to a character in the story but known to the spectator, thereby functioning as a mode of dramatic irony. In *Gone With the Wind*, after Scarlett has been rejected by Ashley and rebuked by Rhett during a party at Twelve Oaks, she stands before a large window. Furrowing her brow and biting her lips, she seems to feel pain and confusion at Ashley's preference for a sweetsop like Melanie over her. The spectator sees her selfishness. Outside the window, over a spacious lawn, a rider comes, adding mobility to a static indoor scene. A woman crosses his path and stops the rider, speaking with him earnestly. Others run across the lawn confusedly. The rider holds fast the reins of his spirited, rearing horse. This background action seems at first to generalize upon Scarlett's confusion, but the spectator soon realizes that some public event has taken place. The image box has introduced pictorially the statement that the Civil War has started. Later, in the same scene, when someone *tells* Scarlett about the beginning of the war, Scarlett thinks aloud: "What do I care about your war! Ashley! Oh, Ashley!" The background action is metaphorical because it parallels the confusion that Scarlett, in close-up, feels; it is an irony because while introducing a fact it also reveals the selfishness of the heroine, who cannot see the importance of a public event which soon enough impinges upon her private life.

In *On the Waterfront* (1954) Elia Kazan uses metaphor as dramatic irony. It is well known that story ideas put into cinematic terms require settings that show movement. A cliché of moviemaking involves "traffic in the background" when two actors perform their scene in a taxi-cab, and the director shows the traffic through the rear window to keep the film moving. Generally the moving cars have no bearing on the foreground action; they show *mere* mobility. When Terry Malloy (Marlon Brando) and his brother (Rod Steiger) are riding, the taxicab has closed Venetian blinds over the rear window, which shut out the conventionally mobile traffic. The drawn blinds create suspicion on the part of the spectator that all will not be well (Fig. 19). In addition to

Courtesy of Columbia Pictures

Fig. 19. *On the Waterfront* (1954). The drawn Venetian blinds of a moving taxi.

serving as a metaphor for intrigue and ignorance, the blinds also serve as a means of irony because they give the spectator information about the taxicab of which the protagonist seems unaware. Throughout the ride, Terry reveals his frustrated hopes for a career in the ring and shows cause for his rebellion against the gang that made him throw a fight. But because Terry has betrayed the gang, his brother will be killed. The spectator is not surprised when the taxicab enters a subterranean garage where the murder will take place. The image of the Venetian blinds has, therefore, served to create terror and suspicion, emotions that would not have been so intensely evoked by showing the usual background traffic. By supplying the spectator with a premonition not apparently felt by the protagonist, they also help to create dramatic irony.

A window is, of course, not essential for such metaphorically significant background action. Sometimes, as the credits of a film unroll, the scene behind them evokes a theme or creates a feeling. In *From Here to Eternity* (1953) Fred Zinnemann had the problem of translating the mood of the novel into cinematic imagery. In the book James Jones devoted a hundred pages to showing that Prewitt's dilemma—his love of discipline and hatred of army disciplinarians—results in his isolation. As the screen credits of the film version unroll, the foreground action reveals a squad of soldiers drilling in response to a sergeant's commands. From the distance a single soldier walks toward them, his barracks bag on his shoulder. He approaches from the dusk of the background area to the lighted area in the foreground where the squad is drilling. By the time the credits have unrolled, Prewitt's change of company has been shown. His loneliness has been conveyed pictorially by the juxtaposition of the single soldier and the squad and by the movement from dark to light.

As the titles of *A Time to Love and a Time to Die* (1958) unroll —the film is based on Erich Maria Remarque's novel of German suffering in World War II—the spectator sees a lilac bush in four stages: in full bloom, in a strong wind that blows away the buds, completely barren, and, finally, bearing the weight of snow. Taken together with the words of the title, the lilac image comments upon the cycles and enduring qualities of life. This preliminary statement of the image does credit to Douglas Sirk, the director, but subsequent repetitions of it lead to overstatement. During an early scene in late winter near a lake, the heroine tells the hero that heat from exploded bombs has caused a lilac bush beside them to sprout buds prematurely; the hero, drawing a message from this fact, tells the heroine that they must cram a lifetime into his three weeks' furlough. After the heroine has lost her father and is carrying her lover's son, she writes to her lover at the front —he is already dead, though she does not know it—that she has understood what he has meant by his interpretation of the prematurely blooming lilac bush, and that even though he were to die, she would be consoled. Each repetition, by picture and word, of the similarity between the lilac cycle and wartime life conveys the theme imagistically. If excessively repeated, as this image is, the symbol becomes a cliché, and its effectiveness is lost.

Both the simple image and metaphor become surrounded by a complex of associations that often spring from the story or from the interpretation of particular actors. Charlie Chaplin going around a corner reminds Parker Tyler of a sailboat in a wind.[3] While Chaplin's tilting, skidding movement is a movie image, it also suggests a conflict between man and nature, a particular action implying an abstraction and therefore appearing to be symbolic. A simple background of the kind called metaphor may approach symbolic proportions. As Steiner and Marcello stand on Steiner's terrace in *La Dolce Vita* (1960), two searchlights scan a night sky, a visible sign of their quest for self-knowledge (Fig. 20). In another scene the two black sides of the altar canopy merge above them in a parabolic arch to indicate their attempt at spiritual communication (Fig. 21).

In an analysis of one image from *Through a Glass Darkly* (1962),

Courtesy of American International Pictures

Fig. 20. *La Dolce Vita* (1960). Background images: two searchlights.

Courtesy of American International Pictures

Fig. 21. *La Dolce Vita* (1960). Background images: two sides of a baldachin arch.

we can see how the context makes a symbol out of the materials of story and setting. The congenitally insane heroine, who awaits a relapse of insanity, believes that only God, whose existence she doubts, can help her. Nevertheless, in a bare room of the summer house, she senses some strange presence—is it God's?—and repairs to this room during imminent fits. After an intimate scene with her younger brother, she asks to be sent back to the mental hospital; a helicopter is sent for, and she returns again to the bare room to await God's action. When she believes the moment of revelation has come, it is because she has seen a disturbing form through the window. What she sees is the shadow of a many-legged figure descending outside her window. For the heroine awaiting a miracle, the revelation proves, as she says, that "God is a spider." The spectator, however, knows that the form is the shadow of the helicopter. This shadow is a thought-bearing image, a symbol that carries its meaning outside the story into life and into theology. In *Winter Light* (1963), the second film of Bergman's trilogy on Christian faith in modern life, the disillusioned pastor says at one point, "God is a spider," referring to the symbol developed in *Through a Glass Darkly*.

Some details or comparisons have been used so frequently in movies that they are clichés, as vapid in cinematic terms as "happy as a lark" or "green as grass" are in written language. Too many films about city life open with a shot of the New York skyline, with another of a skyscraper seen closer, with the camera craning up the building to a window, and with a third of the interior of an office. A western frequently begins with a lone rider on the range or on the trail. An underworld story sometimes begins with a first shot of an ocean liner, a second of a port-hole, and a third of a seaman hiding heroin in a suitcase.

Furthermore, particular objects often are made into conventional or trite symbols. Pages of calendars blow off, the hands of clocks move, wind blows the leaves from trees (to indicate the passage of time or change of season); rain spatters windowpanes, sea water flows over rocks, rockets burst (to dramatize sexual pleasure); newsprint runs through the press and stops at a headline—these conventional devices are stale unless revitalized. Heroes who die unjustly are sometimes compared to Christ on the Cross. A door sometimes will be used as a background because its paneling may suggest the shape of a cross, and the martyr is made to stand against it. In the last shot of *Blockade* (1938), a pro-Loyalist film of the Spanish Civil War period, the dead hero lies against two beams of the rubble that happen to form the shape of a cross. This cliché may have been acceptable once, but nowadays a movie actor who is portraying despair must be careful about how he raises his arms.

Another cliché involves jets of fluid to indicate sexual climax. As the lovers lie close together, perhaps kissing, a wave breaks against a rock and leaves behind spray and spume. Or, as noted, rain impinges against a windowpane; gradually the rain abates and leaves droplets that ooze along the window. In the movie version of *A Streetcar Named Desire* (1951) Elia Kazan makes a transition from Stanley Kowalski's nighttime rape of Blanche Dubois to a morning scene by means of a large street-cleaning hose spouting water at full blast and dribbling to a halt. The comparison of street-washing and Stanley's orgasm in a rape, apart from its inherent vulgarity, juxtaposes a sexual act and a city scene, a rhetorical device found in the imagery of the poetry of Jules Laforgue and T. S. Eliot. Since it has special relevance to Blanche's psychology, this image adapts a cliché and revitalizes it. Similarly Preston Sturges is able to revitalize the same kind of image by using it for comic effect. In a scene in *The Lady Eve* (1941), as Eve tells her "seventh" husband of her preceding marriages, Preston Sturges intercuts frequently that part of the engine of the locomotive where jets of oil lubricate cylinders.

The sound film provides us with aural as well as visual images. Although the sound track has been most often used to render dialogue necessary to the photoplay or to provide music which creates atmosphere or strengthens mood, imaginative directors have explored its imagistic possibilities. The first step in this direction was the use of nonsynchronous sound, by which an auditory impression might substitute for a visual image.

But this use of sound to identify an object and the force acting upon it is the simplest kind of aural stimulus, what we have in fact called the simple movie image. Film artists realize that sound imagery may be used with the same sophistication as visual imagery, that it may, in other words, function both as metaphor and symbol. In three classics, *City Lights* (1931), *A Nous la Liberté* (1931), and *Miracle in Milan* (1951), the distortions of men's voices form a distinct and satiric sound image. Chaplin blurs the speech of the politician in the park in *City Lights* to indicate vapidness. (Later he builds this device to epic proportions in *The Great Dictator* (1940) when he has Hynkel's pseudo-German harangues evolve into fits of coughing.) In like manner, both Clair in *A Nous la Liberté* and De Sica in *Miracle in Milan* transform sound into derogatory images: each shows two capitalists beginning a discussion by mentioning sums of money but ending by emitting the sounds of barking dogs.

Occasionally, even a noise naturalistically rendered as part of a film's setting may be suddenly thrust into metaphorical prominence. In *On the Waterfront*, while Marlon Brando is telling Eva Marie Saint about his past—facts with which the audience is already familiar—the sounds of the waterfront blot out the words coming from Brando's lips and become a kind of tone poem for the emotions being registered on the face of the actress.

A naturalistic sound may be invested with symbolic significance. In *Young Man with a Horn* (1950), a fictionalized account of Bix Beiderbecke's life, the hero searches for a particular note—"the real high note you hit once in a lifetime." At the end, when he believes he hears it—"Hear that note. They said it didn't exist. It's a good note, clean and sweet"—it is, in fact, the wail of an ambulance come to take him to a hospital. The note he has been seeking is a sound representing death.

The meaning and effect of a movie image, whether auditory or visual, is often established by a series of shots rather than by a single shot, in the same way that tempo frequently develops (as we saw in Chapter Four) not only from movement within the shot but from the "metrical arrangement" of a succession of shots. As in the case of similes and analogies in poetry, the juxtaposition of shot-images often welds two rather mundane images into a startlingly fresh metaphor or symbol. In the following description of a selection of shots from Eisenstein's unproduced film script *Ferghana Canal*, it can be seen that the metaphorical and symbolical relationship between water and masonry is fully established, not by their earlier simultaneous appearance in a single shot (in this case No. 12) but by their being later intercut in a series of separate shots (Nos. 13-75):

12. (*l.s.*)* The lake reflects the domes of the mosque, the shrine, the academy [in the city of Urganj]. . . .
13. (*m.s.*) The intricate pattern of silvery channels dissolves into . . .
[13a] the complex arabesques of the ornamental tiles on the façade of a magnificent mosque. . . .
15. (*l.s.*) Water pours from huge reservoirs. It is caught in jars. . . .
19. (*m.s.*) Gleaming tiled streets are lined with splendid shrines. The crowd, richly robed, moves rhythmically through them.
20. (*m.s.*) . . . Dozing water-carriers. Placidly splashing fountains.
32. (*m.s.*) . . . Tamerlane [enemy of the city] quietly speaks: "Water is the strength of that city. . . . Take away the water from Urganj. . . ."
35. (*m.s.*) The frightened faces of the diggers run past the camera.
38. (fade-in) . . . water trickling from the channels . . .
39. (*m.s.*) . . . the emptied lake . . .
40. (*c.u.*) . . . a shriveled water-skin . . .
44. (*m.s.*) Pits, filled with dry lime. Around them stand perplexed masons, with helplessly hanging hands—there is nothing with which to mix the mortar. In the background slaves are throwing beams behind the broken wall.
59. (*m.s.*) The Emir [who rules the city] looks toward the captives. The captains repeat: "No water to mix the mortar! What are we to do?" . . .
60. (*c.u.*) The Emir tersely commands: "Mix the mortar with their blood."
65. (*c.u.*) A curved knife flashes through the frame. . . .
66. (*c.u.*) The stretched neck of a prisoner.
67. (*c.u.*) Blood drips into a tub. . . .
74. (*c.u.*) Greedy hands hastily mix the dark mortar.
75. (*m.s.*) Beams and stones speedily fill the breech in the wall.[4]

* *l.s.* means "long shot"; *m.s.* means "medium shot"; *c.u.* means "close-up."

In this sequence, the metaphorical statement that water is the lifeblood of the city of Urganj is evolved (with, of course, the aid of titles) by means of a set of shot-images strategically juxtaposed. Although the metaphor is rather literally demonstrated (blood is actually used as a substitute for water), it is further enriched by the feelings attached to the details of water and masonry (tone), the suspenseful historical plot (story), the exotic sights of the city (description), and the socialistic theme which Eisenstein is on the point of developing.

In Chaplin's *Modern Times* (1936) a cliché about conformity in the industrial age comes comically alive merely because it is so literally pictorialized with interlocked images. When, in the opening scene of the film, the camera shows a crowd of people emerging from a subway, then cuts to a moving herd of sheep, then back to the crowd, we laugh at Chaplin's audacity in shaping a platitude from one of the cinema's most poetic simile-making devices—the cross-cut.

Sound images as well as depicted objects may of course be constructed into colorful metaphors by means of juxtaposed shots. An effective example of this occurs in Karel Reisz's *Saturday Night and Sunday Morning* (1961). Angered because his girl closes her front door in his face without kissing him good night, Arthur, the film's protagonist, sends the lid of a garbage can clanging into the alley. This is followed by a cut to Arthur working the next morning at his lathe in the factory accompanied by the same kind of discordant sound. A similar noise thus introduced into the second shot extends Arthur's mood of frustration and therefore becomes a metaphorical representation of his dissatisfaction with his workaday world.

Although the cut—together with its refinements, the cross-cut and the jump-cut—seems to be the most powerful and direct means for juxtaposing images and raising them to the status of metaphor and symbol, the film maker may join imagistic shots together by means of any of the transitional devices named in Chapter Four. He may use the dissolve, the wipe, iris-in/iris-out, fade-in/fade-out, the flip frame, and so on.

As we have implied in previous chapters, only inferior film makers would use these arbitrarily as alternatives to the pure cut merely for the sake of variety. Under what circumstances, then, might a director use the dissolve, the wipe, or the fade, instead of the cut, for better control of his imagery? Both the dissolve and the wipe put images into a close juxtaposition since two images share the same frame momentarily. On the other hand, the fade, while also allowing two images to be juxtaposed, makes the separation sharper: the screen is momentarily blank, without any image projected. Shots 4 and 4a of Eisenstein's *Ferghana Canal* use the dissolve in order to show two aspects of the desert—its aridity and its fertility:

4 (*l.s.*) The infinite sands of the desert . . . Over the words of the song, *dissolve to* . . .
4a (*c.u.*) . . . a spray of delicately flowering bush . . .

It is best that these two images share the same frame momentarily because they are two aspects of one thing, namely, the desert that will be reclaimed by the canal. Eisenstein therefore achieves an opposition of images—a before-after effect, the desert being a wasteland but also a place where flowers, and hence food, can grow.

Like the dissolve, the wipe keeps two images on the same frame momentarily and therefore requires that there be a connection between the scene being wiped off and the one being introduced. In *High and Low* (1963) Kurosawa wipes an elegant room, where an industrialist has come to a decision to pay ransom, with a train, from which the ransom money will be paid, rushing in the direction of the horizontal wipe, i.e., from left to right. This transition therefore unifies two important settings of the story, in that both room and train share the same frame for a moment.

The fade marks the end of a sequence of shots and the beginning of another less closely connected than when the dissolve or the wipe makes the transition. The images juxtaposed may not be in as marked accord or opposition as when the dissolve and the wipe are used.

When imaginatively used to join shots, transitions may actually enrich other levels of the film art. They may help to establish tone, as in the case of *Tom Jones* (see wipe chart, page 60); indicate the direction of the structural line (see page 62); and become a unit in the metric line (since, unlike the abrupt cut-line, they occur in time) (see pages 58–59). Therefore, it is not too surprising that these same devices may not only be used to bring two or more shot-images into a metaphorical or symbolical relationship but may themselves function imagistically. For instance, the clock wipe (wipe chart 79-81, 84-85) does not merely bridge two shots but is itself a metaphor for the passage of time; the flip frame may allude to a topsy-turvy world; the downward wipe (wipe chart 3) may suggest pressure being brought to bear from above. In *The Cabinet of Dr. Caligari* (1919) the iris-in/iris-out technique, with its suggestion of the contractions and dilations of the pupil of the eye, becomes a kind of metaphor for the closing off of the view of external reality and the opening up of the inner world of hallucination.

In 1935 Raymond Spottiswoode in his *A Grammar of the Film* complained that "in the visual simile there is no word for 'like.' "[5] that is, the cut as well as the other transitions mentioned do not unambiguously show comparison between shots. Spottiswoode suggested that one of the transitional devices—say, the fan wipe—be arbitrarily set up as a convention for indicating a visual simile. Movie directors have demonstrated, however, that this is unnecessary, for by carefully controlling all other aspects of a film—its plot, rhythm, tone, and theme—they avoid jeopardizing the simile intention of the juxtaposed shots. In Eisenstein's *Strike* there can be little doubt that the slaughtered bull is related to the fired-upon crowd only as a simile, even though the transitions from one image to the other are merely by means of cuts.

In addition to the metaphor developed within a single shot or established in the context of the imagery of other shots, "running metaphors" are achieved by the repetition of an image throughout a sequence of shots, throughout several related sequences, or throughout the film as a whole. The purpose of this repetition is to unify the varied themes of the film by repeating the same images, or kinds of images, in different contexts.

An example of this may be found in the way in which projectiles and inert structures permeate Antonioni's *La Notte*. The opening scenes of the film image forth an impersonal city. On the streets, the many cars, built to move freely and with speed, serve instead as creeping prisons for their occupants. Antonioni describes a modern hospital as "boldly styled with aluminum fixtures and enormous expanses of glass. Almost monstrous in its perfection, it evokes the picture of flawless and implacable science."[6] The great buildings are intended to be monuments to man's progress, but however high they rise, they do not soar. Just as people are paralyzed captives of the cities they have built, the husband and wife, Giovanni and Lidia, are paralyzed captives of the modern marriage of equal partners they have made. Using cars and buildings as symbols, Antonioni not only implies the lifelessness of this pair, but he also conveys a sensory experience of boredom.

Amid this inertia of the city and the couple, Antonioni depicts projectiles that suggest vitality, movement, and freedom. As Lidia stands against silent surfaces of sidewalk and wall, a low-flying jet streaks by over her head, startling her. When she returns to the house where she and her husband were once poor, but presumably more vital, she passes boys who are fighting, flailing their fists like projectiles. Again she is frightened. Some moments later, she finds other boys who are firing rockets, projectiles that delight her. Whereas the jet plane and the flailing fists seem to Lidia destructive and violent, the rockets, large and powerful scientific toys, represent quickened motion in this general background of dullness, akin to the quickening of one's pulse.

At a party, Giovanni and a strange girl use a woman's compact as if it were a projectile, tossing it back and forth across a floor. This game is a desperate and ineffective attempt to escape boredom. After the party, which has also been unsuccessful in changing the spiritless marriage, Giovanni and Lidia make love in the sand trap of a golf course. This final image is ironical. The choice of a golf course (even unused) for the scene seems in keeping with the imagery—stationary masses and violently moving objects. The choice of the sand trap for their love-making reinforces the captivity they have felt from the beginning. In that final scene the two strains of the imagery form an unresolved spasm of activity, the sexual act itself becoming part of captivity.

In *La Dolce Vita* Fellini takes a commonplace substance—water—and by considering all the meanings traditionally attached to it raises it to a poetic metaphor which helps to bind the rather discrete episodes of the film into a whole. We must remember that this work is essentially a modern morality play in which Marcello, the protagonist, attempts in an aimless way to find happiness according to all the standard procedures: through love, family, religion (both Christian and pagan), culture, sex, alcohol, sadism, and work. His failure in all these areas of experience is further dramatized and unified in the way Fellini takes the conventional associations of water—romanticism, purification, baptism, the origin of life—and converts them into derisive irony in each episode. This tone is set by the very first image of the opening sequence, that of the ruined Roman aqueduct of San Felice. "Two thousand years ago," Fellini explains in the scenario, "these arches brought water to the city, but now there are many gaps where whole sections of the aqueduct have fallen in."[7] The moral and cultural discontinuity and decay of the modern world are thus immediately signalized.

Romanticizations of people and places are mocked throughout by means of water imagery. One of Marcello's early loves, Maddalena, is at first sentimentalized because of her aristocratic background, but later we find her making love to him in a whore's apartment which has literally become a flooded cesspool. In a later scene, Marcello's second idealized love, Sylvia, like Danaë standing in a golden shower——

Courtesy of American International Pictures

Fig. 22.

——entices him to wade with her in the Fountain of Trevi—romantic
Mecca for all tourists in Rome. But just as he joins her and is about to win
the coveted kiss, the fountain is turned off and they stand in the basin
ridiculously exposed to the stare of a curious messenger boy (Fig. 23).
Perhaps the only episode in which the romantic aspects of water are not
mocked or made self-conscious occurs at the Baths of Caracalla—the
night club scene in which the waterfall is allowed to enhance the vitality
of the pagan-like dance.

Fig. 23. *La Dolce Vita* (1960). Marcello and Sylvia in the fountain.

The baptismal and purifying implications of water are also inverted in the film. In regard to the Fountain of Trevi scene previously mentioned (Fig. 23), Fellini ironically remarks in the scenario that Marcello sees Sylvia "as the figure of Eve, fresh and unspoiled in a decadent and sophisticated world," and that in answer to Marcello's plaintive "Sylvia, Sylvia . . . who are you?" she "lifts her hand from the water and holds it over his head, letting the drops fall like a blessing."[8] Just at that moment the fountain is turned off. Later the miracle of the Madonna in the field is exposed as false by a downpour which recalls the wrath of Noah's flood rather than a divine blessing (Fig. 24). And near the end of the film, when the carousing party goes to the sea for the purification they have shunned in the chapel service, they are greeted by the critical eye of a sea monster (Fig. 25).

The final image of the film brings us full circle, for like the view of the Roman aqueduct in the film's opening scene, another image of discontinuity and dislocation is imaged forth in water. As the innocent young girl stands on the beach trying to summon Marcello back to his writing career, "the tide runs swiftly between them and her words are vanquished by the sea" (Fig. 26).[9]

Fig. 24. *La Dolce Vita* (1960). The false miracle in the storm.

Fig. 25. *La Dolce Vita* (1960). The ray and the curious revelers.

Fig. 26. *La Dolce Vita* (1960). The sea behind him, Marcello looks longingly toward the innocent life, now lost.

About light and dark imagery in films a whole volume could be written. Not only are illumination and shadow the very substance of film projection—a pure beam of light interrupted, as it were, by various opaque and translucent configurations—but photographic light values continually transform and enhance the nature of reality.* No other explanation so fully accounts for the audience's fascination during the early days of cinema with the simple screening of a train pulling into a station. This intensification of reality is further dramatized by the fact that the audience sees the images from a darkened auditorium, which is womb-like in its ability to isolate them from other, irrelevant visual sensations. A good film maker is constantly aware that he is using light the ways a painter uses paint to excite optical responses and stir psychological processes.

* The effect is quite different from that achieved by lighting in the theater. For one reason the area and intensity of illumination cannot be so well controlled on the stage as in films, with the film's possibilities of varying focal length and lens openings, and combining artificial with natural light. On the stage the spotlight is often merely a substitute for a film shot—a way of demarcating a "frame" of action—not in itself an image, although occasionally representing an invisible presence.

Yet light and shadow may be exploited as film imagery for reasons other than that they are *perceptual* qualities of the medium. In our discussion of the image box in *From Here to Eternity* (see page 85), we might have also pointed out that as Prewitt moves from the dusky background to the illuminated foreground, he makes the symbolic transition from the dark of the past to the light of the present. Traditionally artists have attached such kinds of *conceptual* feelings to the contrast between light and dark, or black and white, thus utilizing them as symbols. In general, dark stands for ignorance, death, chaos, mystery, superstition, and hell; light, for their opposites.

As in literature and painting, the traditional and paradoxical meanings of light and dark are often used in films—perhaps with more potential effectiveness, since light and dark, as we have pointed out, are the very substance of the medium. When too often identified with a particular object or phenomenon in nature, however, a dark or light sensation runs the serious risk of becoming a cliché. Flashes of lightning, standing for God's judgment, have become by now an irredeemable movie platitude, a facile means of capitalizing on a stock response.

In *The Love of Jeanne Ney* (1927)—a film that is remarkable on many counts—G. W. Pabst at first seems to present a sentimental cliché of light imagery, but immediately controls the bathos by uncovering an irony in the metaphor. When Jeanne awakens in the seedy hotel room after having spent the night with her lover, we see her happy face slowly illuminated by the sunlight coming through the window. The suggested banality is that the full force of her innocent love has just "dawned" on her. But a few moments later, as her lover leads her down the dark stairway, her face is again illuminated. As she searches in astonishment for the light source, the camera reveals that it is the flare from a match struck by the villain Khalibiev as he leads a prostitute up to one of the rooms. The same light reveals his own face as a mask of lust—a countenance more in keeping with the surroundings than the pure, naïve expression of Jeanne's.

In *Warning Shadows: A Nocturnal Hallucination* (1922), the film's director, Arthur Robison, avoided a trite use of the traditional meanings of light and dark imagery both by producing practically all the nuances of illumination and shadow of which the medium was at that time technically capable and by having them at the same time subsume every other aspect of the film—the story, theme, characterization, rhythm, and tone. As Siegfried Kracauer points out, "To a large extent, *Warning Shadows* is nothing but an instinct [psychological] film, which accounts for the marked role assigned in it to the display of lights and shadows. Their marvelous fluctuations seem to engender this extraordinary drama."[10]

There are several basic metaphors in the film, all imagistically conceived in terms of light and shadows. A husband's jealousy of his wife's infidelity is literally projected as "shadows of doubt and suspicion." Some of his fears are real, others are illusory: whereas one of the silhouettes seen by him through the bedroom door and showing his wife and her lover embracing represents the true state of affairs, another silhouette seeming to show three admirers caressing the wife is merely a shadow trick perpetrated by a malicious servant with a candelabrum. Thus a corollary function of the shadow imagery is to indicate that the world of appearances and the world of reality are difficult to distinguish from each other.

Into the household comes a shadow-play puppeteer who immediately sizes up the explosive situation. At first we feel he is mischievously intent upon aggravating the trouble when he increases the suitors' lust by strategically placing the candles behind the diaphanous gown of the dancing wife, and then later heightens the husband's jealousy by manipulating the light to fall on the wife and lover as they are about to hold hands. But the puppeteer's use of the harsh truth of light is merely a prelude to the therapeutic use he will make of shadows, and it is at this point that another metaphor is introduced—that the present casts shadows of future events. This had already been hinted at earlier when the puppeteer's own shadow appeared on the wall before he actually entered the room. It is first specifically imaged forth by the presentation of a Chinese shadow play in which a jealous husband slays his wife's paramour. In order that this prophecy might better take hold in their feelings and imagination, the shadow artist simultaneously hypnotizes all six— the husband, the wife, and the four suitors—and literally moves their shadows forward so that each can mentally follow his own into the world of the subconscious. There ensues a shared hallucination portraying the dire events which will occur if the instinct-possessed six allow their passions to continue to shape their behavior. As the conjuror moves their shadows back to their original position on the floor, the dawn significantly breaks in upon a more mature and enlightened group.

Further nuances of the light-dark imagery are attempted in this work by tinting the film stock with appropriate atmospheric colors. The indoor shots are done in yellow tones characteristic of candlelight, while the outdoor night scene providing a setting for the arrival of the shadow artist is tinted a deep lavender. However, the entire sequence of the "nocturnal hallucination," even though it involves indoor shots, is done in lavender to remind us that it derives from the world of shadows; and the outdoor scene showing the lover departing is rendered as the bright yellow of morning to demonstrate that the light of reason has triumphed over the shadows of dark suspicion and lust. Ultimately the yellow and lavender tints are therefore more than atmospheric; they serve to maintain the delineation of two separate psychological worlds.*

This early use of color in *Warning Shadows* raises the whole question of the imagistic function of color in films. Some screen directors seem to feel that black and white is the only rendition that suits their iconology. Can we imagine the serious, almost allegorical films of Ingmar Bergman, dealing as they do with the essential antitheses of life and death, good and evil, faith and disbelief, rendered in any colors other than black and white? However, according to the Danish director Carl Dreyer, black and white, and shades of gray (which after all was the dominant color used until the discovery of color photography itself), are suitable only for naturalistic films and are of little service to "abstraction . . . in a kind of timeless, psychological realism" (symbolism)—the direction in which he thinks films ought to be moving. He urges that film makers steer away from such drabness and praises the color in *Gate of Hell* (1953):

In the same way as French impressionists were inspired by classical Japanese woodcuts, so Western film directors can learn from the beautiful Japanese film *Gate of Hell*. . . . I believe that the Japanese themselves consider this film naturalistic. Through *our* eyes its style tends towards the abstract. . . .

The colours in *Gate to Hell* have undoubtedly been chosen to a well-prepared plan. The film tells us a great deal about warm and cold colours, about the profound use of simplification. . . .

At present we are moving on cat's paws. We can throw in some pastel shades, pink and light blue, to show we have taste. But, as far as the abstract film goes, taste will not be nearly enough. Artistic intuition and courage is necessary to select and compose contrasting colours, to support the dramatic and psychological contents of a film.[12]

Such a view might seem highly unorthodox, since we usually regard the value of color photography to lie in its power to mirror reality more faithfully. But upon further consideration we can see that representationalism,

---

* Griffith's *Intolerance* (1916) also used tinted film stock to approximate reality and gain emotional values: "Night exteriors are tinted blue; sunny exteriors or lighted rooms are in various tones of yellow; blackness drapes the figures in the Temple of Sacred Fire; the Babylon battle at night is heightened by red flares."[11]

as the sole aim of color, merely corresponds to what we have called the simple photographic image, whereas Dreyer is trying to press color into the service of metaphors and symbols that suggest a psychological ambience.

One further remark by Dreyer indicates that perhaps we are on the threshold of discovering a new dimension for the imagistic use of light values in film—of black and white as well as color. In black-and-white photography the merging of light and shadow into a gray background is used to achieve the realistic effect of depth and distance. However, one might, Dreyer points out, "obtain interesting abstraction by deliberately eliminating atmospheric perspective. . . ." This is, in effect, what Truffaut did in the deliberate, seemingly tintype photography of *Jules and Jim* and what Dreyer himself did in the stark two-dimensionality of his own *Vampyr* (1931). In applying this principle to color, one should, Dreyer argues, "work towards an entirely new image-structure; one should plan one's colour surfaces so as to form one large, many-coloured surface. One should eliminate the conception of foreground, middle distance and background. It is possible that very remarkable aesthetic effects could be obtained in this way."[13] This might, in fact, bring us around to a cinematic method analogous to the work of medieval painters like Giotto, in which natural perspective is forefeited for a form and color whose main iconographical intent is symbol or allegory.

Sometimes the meanings of a group of movie images—visual, sound, or color—may be more than just conventionally or traditionally understood. Rather, they may be so deeply embedded in the collective unconscious or racial memory that the anthropologist or the psychologist is required to explain their recurrence. In his article "The Horse: Totem Animal of the American Films," Parker Tyler offers a witty, often tongue-in-cheek, "anthropological" analysis of the sexual and ritualistic uses of the horse in American films. Throughout works like *My Friend Flicka* (1943) and its sequels, and in *The Outlaw* (1943), Tyler discovers the primitive pattern of the initiation trial and ritual of adolescent boys, repressed homosexuality (since the horse is in Freudian lore generally a phallic symbol), and even traces of Adler's power complex.[14] Naturally such symbolic motifs, if they truly exist in these films, are unintentional and are in fact a manifestation of the film maker's subconscious mind. Who can deny that Marlon Brando's painful walk at the end of *On the Waterfront* suggests Christ's ordeal on the Via Dolorosa or any of the scapegoat myths predating it; yet who can prove that the metaphor was intentional (Fig. 27)?

Fig. 27. *On the Waterfront* (1954):

Fig. 27a. Along the Via Dolorosa.

Fig. 27b. Pietà.

Fig. 27c. Toward the Resurrection.

Obviously Cecil B. De Mille, when he made *Manslaughter* in 1922, may not have been aware that he was capitalizing on the generally accepted demoted image of the Negro. During the course of the film, the "modern" heroine commits manslaughter and goes to prison. To indicate her degradation, in contrast to the many scenes in which her carefree affluence has been shown, De Mille reveals her being forced into a line with a Negro woman prisoner, the only Negro in the film. Although, as we have said, the effect is probably unintentional, the heroine's forced association with the Negro woman serves as a symbol of the nadir of her fortunes, for after the casual encounter, she is on the road to becoming a seemingly benevolent and religious person.

Movie images which arise out of the recesses of the subconscious or out of the collective racial memory may of course be *consciously* engendered by the film artist—especially in this day and age of self-styled psychoanalysts. In Germaine Dulac's *The Seashell and the Clergyman* (1928)—a film made, according to the Museum of Modern Art Catalogue, "at the time when the surrealist movement was heavily under the influence of orthodox Freudianism"—there can be found a great deal of deliberate "phallic, castration, and Oedipal symbolism. . . ." One has only to take a cursory look at books like Lo Duca's *L'Erotisme au Cinéma* to realize that one film maker after another has purposely embodied in his work—often for the sake of sheer sensationalism—such pathological and bizarre modes of behavior as the foot fetish, homosexuality, and necrophilia.[15]

All men dream awake—*chacun songe en veillant*—because the mind conceives its own reality based upon the reality of nature. Like images in the mind's eye, movie images not only reproduce but also reorder the details of life. Movie artists like poets use devices of compression and intensity. An image concentrates and compresses, orders and combines, ideas and emotions. David Riesman, the sociologist, confesses that fantasy, not social record or social reform, gives him pleasure in movies. Movies are controlled dreams, subject, like all art, to unities, particularly to unity of action. Like a poet's diction, a moviemaker's shots must obey principles of order. Film images may be empty or cliché-ridden, but they may also, like a great image of poetry, organize diverse elements of a chaotic world so that for a moment a spectator has the sensations of harmony and plenitude as principles of life.

CHAPTER SIX

Tone and Point of View

Aㅣㅌㅎㅗㅜㄱㅎ cinematography is regarded as the most objective of the arts, because it most directly records reality, it conveys, like other arts, the artist's attitude and feeling. Even when the film maker is trying to be totally objective, as is the case of the newsreel photographer or the documentarist, he can never avoid coloring the film with his own temperament and personality. He may offer the viewer pictures of actual events, hard visual facts, such as a battle, a parade, or an interview; he may show objects, such as the Eiffel Tower, the S.S. *United States,* or a Picasso mural. Yet, however much he considers these materials to be "unmalleable" or presented in a straightforward manner, no filmed object or event is, strictly speaking, unmalleable. Although an object has its naked existence, it also has enormous potential for larger significance. It can be clothed, as it were, in broader meanings, which can be conveyed by the way the object is lighted, or by the angle from which it is seen, or through the context of its presentation. The film maker chooses his lighting, angle, and frame, and even the length of time he will shoot the object. In so doing, he evokes an atmosphere and expresses a style.

Art, no matter what the form or medium or how realistic it attempts to be, works through conventions that are meant to encourage credibility. Perspective and chiaroscuro are devices which establish illusion through convention, so that even the painter who pursues realism must deal with his subject obliquely. In so doing, he is bound to express something of himself. In like manner, the film maker, even when he is filming a true-to-life story, not only provides the authentic setting in which the life was lived but conveys a feeling about that life. Whatever degree of

105

realism is intended, there will be in such a film a complex of attitudes, as embodied in the various characters and in the over-all atmosphere that represents the point of view of the film maker. Thus the film maker not only shows us what he wants us to see but also forces us to react to what he is showing us in the manner that he desires.

The writer of fiction immediately assumes a stance from which to see and judge the persons and events of his story. He may allow both himself and the reader the "aesthetic distance" afforded by third person narration—that is, the point of view of the omniscient author; or he may try to get the reader to identify more closely with what is going on by using the first-person narration—that is, having a character recount the events.

Some definitions are in order. The attitudes expressed in film may be objective, as in newsreels; subjective, as when the audience sees the world from the point of view of a character; or objective-subjective, as when the director intermixes objective and subjective shots in order to impose his own attitude on the film the audience is seeing. *Point of view*, therefore, refers to whether the filmed material purports to be unmalleable reality (objective) or reality as seen by a character (subjective). *Attitude* is the film maker's manipulation of objective and subjective shots in order to reveal his meaning. *Tone* is the attitude of the film maker both toward his filmed material and toward the audience with which he is communicating. Tone involves the film maker's and the audience's feelings of pleasure and pain, or their mixed feelings; their belief in the truth of what is on the screen; their awareness of whether the mixture of objective and subjective shots creates a style that is straightforward or ironical.

Because the movie camera can move and "see" the way a character in a film would, it allows film makers to use a first-person point of view. The camera "walks" by dollying; it raises or lowers its "head" by tilting; it surveys a scene by panning or climbs and descends by "craning"; it gets dizzy by swish-panning and faints by going out of focus. When such effects as these are consciously exploited throughout the film we get an effect known as "subjective camera." In films containing hospital scenes, the world is often seen from the point of view of the patient as he is rushed to or from the operating room. Often we see only the lights of the ceiling rushing by, or the faces of those walking by seen from a "subjective," upward angle. And usually when the patient awakens from an operation the camera lens is made gradually to change the face of the attending doctor or nurse from a soft blur to a sharp focus. In fact, such use of the subjective camera has become a convention for scenes in which a person regains consciousness. On a more vigorous plane, when lovers are shown in a swoon of passion, the camera loses focus and the pictures fade out. (The ego is often made identifiable by clarity of registration while the forces of "unreason" are suggested by the camera's being off focus.) When it seems that the audience can be induced to identify most completely with the character undergoing stress, as when losing consciousness, the film director will shift to this kind of subjective point of view.

Also conventional is the trick of placing the camera on fast-moving vehicles upon which characters are supposedly traveling in order to "subjectify" their kinesthetic sensations. In *Entr'acte* (1924) René Clair, in anticipation of Cinerama, placed the camera on a moving roller coaster. He frightens and dizzies the spectator even more by keeping the camera upside down. E. A. Dupont made the audience share the kinesthetic sensations of the acrobats of *Variety* (1926): for the death-defying trapeze act, he placed a camera on one of the swinging trapezes and intercut that perspective of the action with objective shots of the performers doing their routine. A similar effect was achieved during the fox hunt in *Tom Jones* when a camera was mounted on a running horse to approximate Tom's experience more closely.

The very rate at which movement is photographed can be used artistically to suggest moods and the workings of a character's mind. If the camera's rate is slowed as it photographs a moving object, the projection of the film at normal speed will make the action seem accelerated; for the contrary effect, if the camera's rate is speeded up, the movement of the projected image appears as slowed down. Very frequently this second phenomenon (slow motion) is used to suggest a surrealistic dream or an entire emotion-laden memory going on in a character's mind. One of the most effective of these occurs in the boy's dream in Buñuel's *Los Olvidados* (*The Young and the Damned*) (1950). The sight of the mother coming to give her son a piece of raw meat and bestow her affection upon him is made peculiarly nightmarish by her approach in slow motion. Another instance is the vision experienced by the protagonist in Lindsay Anderson's *This Sporting Life* (1963) as his team slowly and unrelentingly scrimmages in the mud. Here the gruesome tone is enhanced by complete silence on the sound track and a twilight effect in the lighting. In both these cases the antigravitational effect of the slow motion seems particularly appropriate to the uninhibited nature of the memory or dream.

Other cinematic methods of pictorially rendering a subjective dream or memory consist of the photographic superimposition of images—involving double printing—or a flash-back shot. Usually the subjective sequences are recapitulations of a character's previous experiences rather than surrealistic distortions of them. In *The Birth of a Nation* (1915) Margaret Cameron "sees in her imagination the death of her second brother, *Wade* . . . killed during the battle of Atlanta."[1] A balloon vignette of Wade appears. He lies prostrate on the earth near a fence, refugees streaming past him, and he closes his eyes in death.

The superimpositions we are speaking about show the memory and the rememberer simultaneously and therefore convey a subjective tone—the attitude of the rememberer being activated by the pictures printed with him, as when a man huddling in the cold "dreams" of a warm hearth and his wife and children surrounding him. Griffith often had the reminiscing character stare off into space and then showed in the same shot the remembered person or object or event framed in an iris, perhaps against a solid background. Strictly speaking, the flash back is also a storytelling device in which events are presented out of a time sequence, but with the pictures of past experiences interrupting pictures of the present. Thus in *The Girl Who Stayed at Home* (1918), Robert Herron, portraying a civilian weakling nicknamed "Slouchy," is provoked to action by a memory picture from his past. When Trüberein, a bully in the small town, sees Slouchy with a girl, the bully beats him off, embarrassing him. During World War I, after the army has made a man of him, Slouchy recognizes Trüberein as the enemy German approaching him for single combat. In order to show what Slouchy is thinking, Griffith cuts to the scene in the park where Slouchy was beaten up (a flash back) and cuts back to the revenge of Slouchy, who now knocks out Trüberein.

Other interesting photographing and editing principles have been used to pictorialize characters' mental states or imaginings. The "flash shot," almost subliminal in its effect since it consists of only a few frames, has been used by avant-gardist Gregory Markopoulos in *Twice a Man* (1963), by Alain Resnais in *Last Year at Marienbad* (1962), and by Joseph Strick in *Ulysses by James Joyce* (1967) to represent flashes of memory. In *Marienbad* an increased lens aperture in one of these shots causes an intensification of light, underlining the climax of the man's memory of running toward the woman. Jan Kadar in *The Shop on Main Street* (1965) uses intensified light along with distorted motion for two "dream" sequences—the man and woman at one point seeming to glide, at another moving with exaggerated slowness. Again, after the protagonist has killed the Jewish woman, the camera at first behaves subjectively, that is, simulates his eye movements by "looking around" the shop, and then seems to become his antagonist as it presses in on him accusingly. In the latter case the camera is endowed with the moods of the participant.

Another frequently used method of shifting to subjective camera is that of exaggerating camera angles. Films featuring children as principal figures may abound in low-angle shots of adults because the director may wish to remind the audience frequently of the perspective of a child's reality. In Carol Reed's *The Fallen Idol* (1949) we are often reminded that adult experiences are affecting the sensibilities of a small boy. This is accomplished through low-angle shots of their behavior as he observes them. Likewise, in a sequence from Laughton's *The Night of the Hunter*, a low-angle shot of Robert Mitchum looming up over the children as he pursues them into the water combines a realistic presentation of their low angle of vision with a more expressionistic indication of their nightmarish awareness of his overpowering force. A similar device was used by David Lean in *Great Expectations*: the angle enables Magwitch to appear suddenly hovering over the frightened Pip. In Nicholas Ray's *Bigger Than Life* (1955), a man made megalomaniac by excessive use of cortisone says, "I feel ten feet tall," and the camera shoots him from a low angle.

Very rarely does a film maker seek to sustain throughout the entire film a subjective tone from the point of view of one of the characters. *Lady in the Lake* (1947) is an exceptional instance in which this is attempted. In this film the detective-hero is not photographed but is "experienced" only through the flexible moving eye of the camera. Occasionally we see his hands or arms reach up into the bottom of the frame, and several times we even see his reflection in a mirror. But these are not really violations of the subjective camera or first-person point of view because a person is always capable of seeing "objectively" parts of his own body or his own mirror image.

In the theater, the principal means—perhaps the *only* means—open to the playwright who wants to achieve considerable subjectivity in the viewpoint of a character is expressionism. Thus in Elmer Rice's *The Adding Machine* the set designer must plaster the walls with huge numerals in order to project the state of mind of the accountant-protagonist.

It is interesting to compare such an effort on the stage with a similar highly reputed one on the screen—*The Cabinet of Dr. Caligari*. At the end of the film the audience discovers that the wild distortions in the design of the painted sets represent projections of an insane mind. Film historians have often observed that *Caligari*, despite its effectiveness, is both the alpha and omega of expressionism in films, but few have said precisely why. The answer is probably that the film's expressionistic devices were theatrical and not cinematic. The camera itself, through such functions as angle, movement, and focus, could have more effectively created the mad doctor's subjective view of the world which in the theater is almost the sole province of the set designer.

Not all shifts to the subjective camera are as dramatic as those accomplished by moving the camera in exceptional ways or placing it in exceptional positions, blurring or sharpening its focus, placing it on fast-moving vehicles, or varying its rate of speed or light intensity as it photographs.

Frequently the switch from an omniscient "third-person" point of view to a "first-person" one is so unobtrusive that the audience is not conscious of it. This is partly because no unorthodox camera techniques are used but, even more likely, it is because the change is mandatory for continuity. A shot framing a character looking at something off screen naturally arouses an expectation in the audience that the succeeding shot will show what the character is looking at. The first of these, what Vorkapich calls the "look of outward regard," indicates that a character is looking at something. The second, called an "eye-line shot," is what he sees. Even though the latter may not involve an impressionistic visualization (as shown, say, by the blurred focus or low camera angle) and though it therefore may seem to be merely fulfilling the objective requirement of continuity, it is subjective in that it stands for what the character sees.

If the director forgets that a shot containing a "look of outward regard" almost inevitably requires that the next shot will be a subjective view of what is seen, he runs the risk of creating a confusion or absurdity. For instance, Vorkapich holds that in *L'Avventura*, when Antonioni follows a shot of Monica Vitti looking up to a bedroom window with a supposedly objective shot of a couple making love inside, we momentarily feel that the second scene represents her voyeuristic observance of the pair—an impression not intended. If the "objective" shot is from Antonioni's point of view, the first has falsely prepared the spectator for a subjective, eye-line shot. Or when Flaherty, in *Man of Aran* (1934), photographs a woman gazing through a window (she remarks that her husband is seven days out at sea) and then follows this with a middle shot of fishermen sitting in boats, the audience for a moment has the mistaken notion that the second shot dramatizes some incredible power in the woman to see many miles out to sea. But, like Antonioni, Flaherty ignores the rule, and entertains poetic, or cinematic, license by abruptly shifting from the point of view of the character to his own, imposing his own feelings on the sequence. Antonioni willfully uses cinematic license because he is astonished by the free sensuality of the couple who make love knowing that Monica Vitti is waiting for them; Flaherty is willing to confuse the audience momentarily in order to regale the moviegoer with the power of the cinema to take the journey from the woman to the men at sea, a journey that the woman cannot take. Both Antonioni and Flaherty intermix objective and subjective shots in order to convey their own attitudes.

As we have seen, a shift to the subjective camera seems both reasonable and desirable when a character gets caught up in an intense or exciting experience or when his "eye line" is directed off camera. Like first-person narration in fiction, the subjective shot not only dramatizes a character's or film maker's attitude or point of view but involves the spectator more intimately in the action. In other words, even though the moviegoer remains aware that he is observing the emotional reaction of a separate character, the subjective camera at the same time impels him into the shock or delight of an immediate experience.

Frequently the subjective camera technique may secure the spectator's participation in an event without there being any portrayal of a character to share the emotional involvement. Cinerama, which employs such tricks as placing a camera on a roller coaster, is an obvious contemporary example of this, for here the camera does not represent a character who is part of a fiction but attempts to substitute for the filmgoer himself. In the same way, camera angles, besides expressing the point of view of a particular character, as in *The Fallen Idol*, may be a direct invitation from the film maker to the audience to share in his own attitude or feeling. When Murnau in *The Last Laugh* has his camera "look up" at the old doorman's good fortune by means of low-angle shots, and later makes it "look down" at his misery with high-angle ones, he is not only enhancing the tragic reversal, but is imposing upon us—perhaps without our awareness or conscious consent—attitudes of reverence, condescension, and social judgment of a sort. When Ozu, often called the most Japanese of Japan's film directors, insists on shooting almost all his scenes with the camera elevated only three feet from the floor, he is supposedly forcing all of us to maintain a Japanese out-look, for according to film critic Iwasaki Akira,

> Ozu's reasoning . . . is as follows: the Japanese people spend their lives seated on "tatami" mattings spread over the floor; to attempt to view such a life through a camera high up on a tripod is irrational; the eye-level of the Japanese squatting on the "tatami" becomes, of necessity, the level for all who are to view what goes on around them; therefore the eye of the camera must also be at this level.[2]

There are of course other less subtle types of "audience participa-tion" films involving the subjective camera. In *Tom Jones* the characters occasionally wink at or address the camera (i.e., the audience). Tom at one point virtually accuses it of pruriently peeking at Mrs. Waters' semi-nudity by clapping his hat over the lens; at another point he brands it phlegmatic when in jubilation at Allworthy's recovery he tears down the black drapes to "cover first the pious ones [Blifil, Thwackum, Square, and Dowling], then the screen."[3] The detached, comical tone achieved by Richardson springs from intermixed objective and subjective shots. However, a director may have no purpose in shifting from one camera angle to another. He may be achieving nothing more than cinematic coherence, as when Cukor in *Rhapsody* (1954) achieves a visual balance by shooting all sequences of a violinist from below and all those of a pianist from above.

The film maker may withdraw from the material by allowing the actors to perform or events to occur as if he were not manipulating them, or even present, or he may introduce himself by self-conscious technique —variable camera distance, space play, or masking—with a great degree of involvement. Through his style, he intrudes himself and therefore his attitude, unwilling to allow the actors and the story to "roll" by without his "comment."

Within the third-person, objective point of view, there are degrees of self-consciousness. To some of the early readers of novels the device of the omniscient narrator itself must have seemed strange, since it is unreal for a reporter of events to know what every character is thinking or doing. Homer and Virgil overcame this potential awkwardness by pretending that their knowledge and inspiration came directly from an all-knowing, all-seeing muse. However, some of the early English nov-elists like Fielding did not seek to make the "unreality" of the conven-tion unobtrusive, but on the contrary capitalized for comic effect on their readers' awareness of the narrator's omniscience and omnipresence.

Fielding's tone was that of a creator delighted to present and control his puppets but frequently lapsing into mock horror and disavowal of responsibility as their immoral behavior led them to take on a life of their own. Thus the comedy was partly achieved by the author's reminding us of his role and insisting upon a tone of detachment and of moral and aesthetic distance.

By what special cinematic devices can a film maker establish this same tone of comic detachment through a third-person narrator? Tony Richardson's film version of *Tom Jones* provides some interesting insights into the more palpable uses of the camera as self-conscious narrator.

Although Richardson used the voice of a narrator (a surrogate of Fielding) on the sound track, a total reliance on this device would obviously have been verbal and literary rather than cinematic. Fortunately Richardson did not attempt a literal transcription of the novel, but found suitable movie substitutes, principally in order to equalize in cinema the humorous tone which we recognize as mock-heroic. Many of these consisted of revivals of archaic artifices, such as the wipe (in every possible variation),* stop photography, photoanimation, and accelerated action. The continual intrusion of these almost forgotten techniques (particularly the fancy wipes) is a constant reminder of the "author's" presence, control, detachment, and bemusement.

Part of our delight in comedy is the sight of someone caught in a mechanistic order of existence. The art of the cinema, dependent as it is upon a complex and ingenious machine, is aptly suited for the creation of such a tone. In *Tom Jones* Richardson accomplishes this kind of farcical effect several times. In the bedroom farce at the inn, involving Mrs. Waters, for example, people are reduced to frantic, scurrying insects because the action is greatly accelerated—a standard comic technique going back to the earliest days of film making. Strangely enough, speeded action seems more rigidly confined to expressing a farcical tone than is slow motion in expressing serious feelings. Accelerated motion resists being used for tones other than farcical. In *Nosferatu* (1922)

---

* When Richardson editorializes in the manner of Henry Fielding, his intrusive wipes underline his attitude. As Tom and Molly Seagram are about to make love in the woods, he censors the scene with a wipe (see wipe chart, Fig. 15, No. 10) which resembles the closing of sliding doors, and when he returns to the censored scene, he uses its opposite (Fig. 15, wipe No. 9). A discreet amount of time is presumed to have passed.

Richardson uses the spiral wipe (Fig. 15, No. 51) to show Tom ecstatic in his new London clothes and a bar wipe (Fig. 15, No. 106) to introduce the actual bars of the prison in which Tom is confined.

Murnau shot the journey of the vampire's carriage and later the loading of the coffins into the wagon in fast motion in order to indicate the villain's supernatural powers, but succeeded only in making these amusing rather than frightening.

Another incident in *Tom Jones* involves an entirely different technique for achieving a mechanical mode of comic behavior while emphasizing the mock-heroic tone of the film maker. While Tom is recovering from a broken arm, he engages in donkey riding. By means of "stop photography" Richardson is able to make it appear as if Tom follows himself in a procession. The effect is that of a merry-go-round composed of several Joneses on donkeys.

Most of the self-conscious techniques used by Richardson for aesthetic distance in *Tom Jones* had first been revived from films of three or four decades ago by Truffaut in his *Jules and Jim*, which contained additional intrusive elements like an intentional graininess in texture to suggest tintype photographs. These conventions are becoming so widespread in television commercials that they are losing their quaintness and with it their suggestion of a critical distance between the artist and his creation.

Sometimes a startling tone is created by accident, whether due to lighting or to interruption. A news photographer may begin to film objectively but discover that the product is enlivened by accidental circumstances. When the camera finds itself reacting impulsively, as it were, to an unpredictable situation, newsreels and *cinema vérité* may reach their epitome of dramatic effectiveness. In the frequently shown footage of the moments immediately following the assassination of President Kennedy in Dallas the camera swings confusedly, searching about for the source of the trouble, passing over the fearful bystanders throwing themselves to the ground, then to a policeman drawing his gun, then to the speeded-up motorcade—the street all the while seeming to tilt at crazy angles as the photographer seeks to aim the camera. In retrospect the cameraman, originally interested only in making a newsreel of the procession, probably regretted his lack of aplomb and professional control over his machine. But the excited quality of the filming, despite its amateurishness, caught the emotional impact of the incident in a way that might have been impossible under the conditions of cool professionalism.

In the "News on the March" sequence in *Citizen Kane*, Orson Welles at one point anticipates *cinema vérité* technique in order to emphasize the rarity of a glimpse of Kane's seclusion in his later years.

The camera which captures the inaccessible tycoon being wheeled about in the garden of a private sanitarium seems to move surreptitiously from behind a tree and to record with some haste and difficulty. (The rest of the "News on the March" sequence, a parody of the "March of Time" series, is done in traditional newsreel style: highly mannered in its spoken commentary and well planned in its camera arrangements.) In this instance we have a highly conscious camera technique masquerading as an impulsive, unplanned style, as if it were on the spot like the camera that filmed Kennedy's assassination.

In George Landow's "loop film" entitled *This Film Will Be Interrupted After Eleven Minutes for a Commercial* (see Chapter 4, page 61) the ultimate in self-consciousness is achieved, although not by camera techniques but by a special process of photographic printing and projection. Landow calls attention to all the mechanical aspects of film projection of which the audience is not supposed to be aware, or becomes aware of only during a faulty projection, and seeks to transform them into a meaningful aesthetic experience. This is comparable to a cultivated self-consciousness in other art forms—in the theater, for instance, when Pirandello, Wilder, or Genêt has characters directly address the audience to remind them that they are in a theater, or in architecture when the architect allows the skeleton of his structure to protrude in order to become an integral part of the effect. In Landow's loop the self-consciousness of technique seems designed to direct our attention away from subject matter and into a kinesthetic involvement with the film's rhythm and movement.

Supposedly the diametric opposite of using camera and projector for aesthetic self-consciousness is *cinema vérité*, or direct cinema, which aims at recording the completely spontaneous, or only partly improvised, "happening." This is made possible by the light and mobile hand-held camera, which the operator can easily thrust into intimate situations and hope for the "gift" or accident of something spontaneously beautiful or inherently exciting. The following is a description of one of the more successful pioneering efforts in this movement:

Desistfilm [by Stan Brakhage] employs all the techniques of a spontaneous cinema. It describes a wild party held by a young group of youths, with all their youthful exhibitionisms, adolescent games and adolescent love images, and was shot in one evening at a real improvised party with a 16 mm camera, most of the time hand-held, following every movement wildly, without any premeditated plan. This technique of the freed camera enabled him to recreate the mood and tempo of the party, with all its little details of foolish, silly, marginal actions, its outbursts of adolescent emotions. The camera, freed from its tripod, gets everywhere, never intruding, never interfering; it moves into close-ups, or follows the restless youths in fast, jerky tilts and pans. There seems to be a perfect unity here of subject matter, camera movement, and the temperament of the film maker himself. The free flight of life has been caught, and the film has vitality, rhythm, and also the temperament of a poem by Rimbaud, of a naked confession—all improvisation, with no artist's hand visible.[4]

While the director can make us conscious of his technique in order to retain "editorial" control of what his audience feels, he also can more subtly manipulate audience reaction by his choice of camera distances. Close shots, which peer at objects, create intensity; long shots, by their distance, imply detachment. During a television interview in 1964, French film maker Jean-Luc Godard made the rather startling statement that "tragedy is close-up and comedy is long shot,"[5] but that he often took pleasure in reversing these in his own films. The resultant tone reflects Godard's tragicomic view of life.

What does the first part—the traditional part—of this statement amount to essentially? If we think of a Chaplin film like *City Lights*, we remember that most of the farcical scenes are shot roughly within the range of middle to long shot. Since Chaplin's comic art is mainly one of bodily movement (including acrobatics and the dance), we can understand why this is necessary. In contrast, when we recall scenes of strong pathos in *City Lights*, as when the previously blind girl recognizes the tramp as her benefactor, the close-up shot of Chaplin's face seems necessary to convey the heartfelt emotions registered there.

Since it is generally true that film comedy consists mainly of people interacting in a physical way with objects or each other and that the principal physiological movement at times of grief is facial, Godard's assumption about traditional cinema seems true. However, in the examples mentioned above the camera functioned more as a recorder of the emotion than as a creator of it. Many film makers, including Godard himself, are not content merely to use variable focal lengths as an optical convenience but rather insist on using it to signal a tone.

In reminiscing about two of his films—*Long Day's Journey into Night* (1962) and *A View from the Bridge* (1961)—Sidney Lumet remarked that close-ups were a predominant feature of the first film whereas some extremely long shots had been used with particular purpose in the latter film. Since both are tragedies and both are adaptations from stage plays, the contrasts in camera distance are noteworthy. Lumet felt that the many close-ups he used in *Long Day's Journey* helped to convey the sense of confinement and entrapment the protagonist suffers in the heart of his family. But perhaps more importantly his use of close-ups allowed him to make Katharine Hepburn's face the real playing area in the film. To the extent that tragic emotions, being movements of the *psyche*, are most clearly registered in the face, this seems entirely appropriate. In *A View from the Bridge*, close-ups are also helpful in establishing the crowded conditions in the tiny Brooklyn apartment, especially after the arrival of the immigrants Marco and Rodolfo. But these scenes are not climactic in that they are not part of Eddie's tragic ordeal of personal loneliness and eventual alienation from the community. The actual intensity of Eddie's plight is emphasized in at least three memorable long shots.

The first of these occurs when Eddie, jealous of the two lovers Rodolfo and Catherine, follows them on their first visit to Manhattan. Eddie's painful separation from the shared intimacy of the young pair as they enjoy the bright lights of Times Square and the Automat is enhanced by his and our long-shot views of them. (Greater lateral distances are also made possible by the wide screen.)

During this sequence Lumet sometimes achieves a tragicomic effect because the use of a deep-focus lens allows both a close-up and long-shot within the same shot. In one of these, in which we see Eddie in the foreground observing the happy cavorting couple in the background, the long shot of the pair allows us detached amusement, while the close-up of Eddie's pained face forces us into compassion for his suffering.

The second significant long shot is an overhead crane shot of Marco and Eddie fighting in the street. Here it is important that we see the broad area of pavement which separates the contenders from the circle of neighbors who are willing to watch but not become involved. While the overhead position of the camera intensifies the tragedy of Eddie's isolation, the distance of the camera and the encompassing view it affords invite us to view the struggle as a kind of "human comedy."

One of the final long shots of the film is done in deep focus to establish even another significant facet of the tragic tone of the film. In the distant background we clearly see the crowd now huddled around Eddie's dead body. A great expanse of empty street (its vastness intensified by the camera's low angle) connects the background group with a phone booth in the foreground. During this shot, Alfiere, Eddie's lawyer-friend and a kind of Greek chorus in the film, detaches himself from the crowd and comes forward across the pavement to the phone booth to report the death to the police (and to us). Here the mood is almost identical with a Greek tragedian's discretion in keeping violent death at a distance and sending a messenger forward to report it.

Although in general the dictum that close-ups are suitable for tragedy and long shots are likely to be used in comedy is sound, we have already demonstrated that it is not universally true, any more than is the use of slow motion solely for seriousness. Whereas tragedy frequently demands of an audience the kind of personal involvement afforded by close-ups and comedy demands the kind of detachment conveyed by long shots, the distant shots of Eddie in the last scene of *A View from the Bridge* were nevertheless tragic.

In like manner, a close-up for comic rather than tragic effect might be illustrated in a scene from *The Idle Class* (1921). We are first given a middle-close-up of the back of Chaplin's head and shoulders heaving in great agitation. Since the audience has just been shown his wife's telegram stating that she has left him in protest against his drinking, it assumes that the movement is caused by weeping. But when he turns toward the camera Chaplin is shaking a cocktail. The middle-close-up of the blankness of his expression—where moviegoers expected to see his face as a "playing area" alive with the emotions of grief—becomes a delightful comic surprise.

But what special tone does Godard achieve by a willful inversion of the usual formula? If we examine the camera distance in certain shots of *A Woman Is a Woman* (1961) and *My Life to Live* (1962) we notice that he achieves the special complexity of tragicomedy or dark comedy. In the latter film, the opening shots of the couple sitting at the coffee bar are "tragic" in that the man and woman are discussing the break-up of a serious marriage, but as close-ups the shots are at the same time "humorous" because the camera keeps panning the totally unrevealing backs of their heads.

A Woman Is a Woman is on the surface a musical comedy but reverberates with undertones of the pain of serious emotional commitments. One of the most noticeable oddities of the film is that the musical "production" numbers, traditionally (as in Fred Astaire musicals) shot in medium-long shots, are frequently done in close-up. Here it would seem that Godard is not so much inverting the use of close-ups for comic incongruity as he is leading us through them from the obvious farcical tone to a sense of what Sarris calls "the exquisite agony of heterosexual love."[6] The intimacy of the woman's sexual wiles, as she tries to maneuver her lover to give her a child; the subtlety and ambivalence of her feelings of moral indiscretion in getting her lover's friend to seduce her; the signs of her contrition and her lover's forgiveness; and the wink with which she asserts the irresistible urge of a woman to procreate must all be conveyed through close-ups.

Facial close-ups frequently stress the intimacy and eroticism of a love scene. This tradition extends all the way from Edison's close-up of John Rice and May Irwin in *The Kiss* (1896) to Warhol's tight shots of Naomi Levine with various males in *Kiss* (1964). Avant-garde film makers Willard Maas and Stan Brakhage have perhaps pushed the close-up technique to its ultimate limits for eliciting erotic overtones. In his *Geography of the Body* (1954) Maas achieves half-erotic, half-humorous effects by photographing in close-up some of the sexually neutral parts of the body, like the ear, in such minute detail that our loss of the usual perspective makes them appear as a genital organ, breast, or anus. In *Loving* (1956), Brakhage, by moving the camera so rapidly and in such myopic close-up over parts of arms, faces, and shoulders of the two lovers, prevents us from achieving a proper "gestalt" of what we are seeing and thus stimulates us to imagine that we might be observing some "forbidden" body area or movement.

The tonality that the film maker achieves through variable camera distances may be reinforced by the way he composes a shot. By varying camera distance he in fact reorganizes the lines and masses within the frame. For instance, a dark tree on a plain photographed in long shot against a bright sky would blot out less than one percent of the light mass. When registered in middle shot it might occupy one-third of the area; when moved to close-up, perhaps 90 percent. Furthermore, if the camera lens "zooms" the tree from long range to close range, the tree appears to grow because the vertical line of the tree lengthens while the horizontal line caused by the meeting of sky and plain and already extending the full length of the screen remains constant. Thus the film maker creates certain subtle feelings of exhilaration, heaviness, flight, despair, excitement, and so on, not only by the change in distance but by the shift or "play" in the proportion and balance of masses, planes, and lines.

In producing atmosphere and mood by such means film makers are merely giving a more dynamic quality to principles of composition long exercised in painting and still photography. Masses with a predominance of strong horizontal lines, especially if shot from a low angle, establish a feeling of heaviness, quietness, and confinement. The wide flight of the Odessa Steps shot from below in *Potemkin*, or the filming of the "fat man" (Sidney Greenstreet) in black clothes and from a low angle in

The Maltese Falcon, achieves effects of awesome massiveness. In contrast, the accentuation of vertical lines tends to produce feelings of festivity, freedom, and perhaps soaring inspiration. Church spires, Gothic vaults, trees, and flagpoles, whether symbolically significant or not, may give these impressions, especially when surrounded by large lighted areas.

When diagonal lines stretch across the screen they frequently bring an effect of liveliness and an expansion of movement, especially if they join foreground to background. Waves washing onto a shore will easily produce these effects if the beach line is made to run diagonally across the screen. Circular lines and scattered dots tend to produce a sparkling, happy, fluttering impression (freedom from inhibition because free of structural cohesion or centrality). A memorable overhead shot of the Beatles cavorting on a football field in *A Hard Day's Night* is a case in point. Aerial shots of a terrain dotted by bombardments from an aircraft are joyous regardless of what one's attitudes toward war are supposed to be, as is the accompanying shot of Parisians in *Le Joli Mai* (1963) pictured from above at a great distance and separated by great patches of light (Fig. 28).

Naturally the structural lines and volumes of masses rarely work alone to produce tonal effects. Balances and imbalances of light and darkness, as just noted, harmonies and disharmonies of planes, dynamism of movement within and between shots are usually crucial as visual complements. Witness, for instance, the following description of how the heavy mood in *The Late Mattia Pascal* (1924) is brought about:

> Cavalcanti, who conceived the settings for Marcel l'Herbier's psychological fantasy after Pirandello, *The Late Mattia Pascal,* has not only set the prevailing mood, but has foreshadowed the entire action of the piece by his emphasis on line and plane, his architectural and decorative distortions. By using heavy shadows and dizzying designs, by distortions of plane and surface, he has underscored the rhythms of this strange, distorted tale of Pirandello's imagining. [See Fig. 29.] The long lines of the windows, the abrupt and jagged geometric pattern of the carpet, the heaviness of the Gothic arches, the very artificiality of the studio lighting, are all used to exaggerate the note of morbid unreality of the drama.[7]

In the accompanying still from *Sweet and Sour* (1963) (Fig. 30), we see that lightheartedness and joyful movement are suggested not only by tall thin trees and the waving diagonal line of the shore, but also by the preponderance of white over black, the smooth texture of the ice, the spotted effect of the leaves above, the softness of the focus, and presumably by the dynamic movement of the figures themselves.

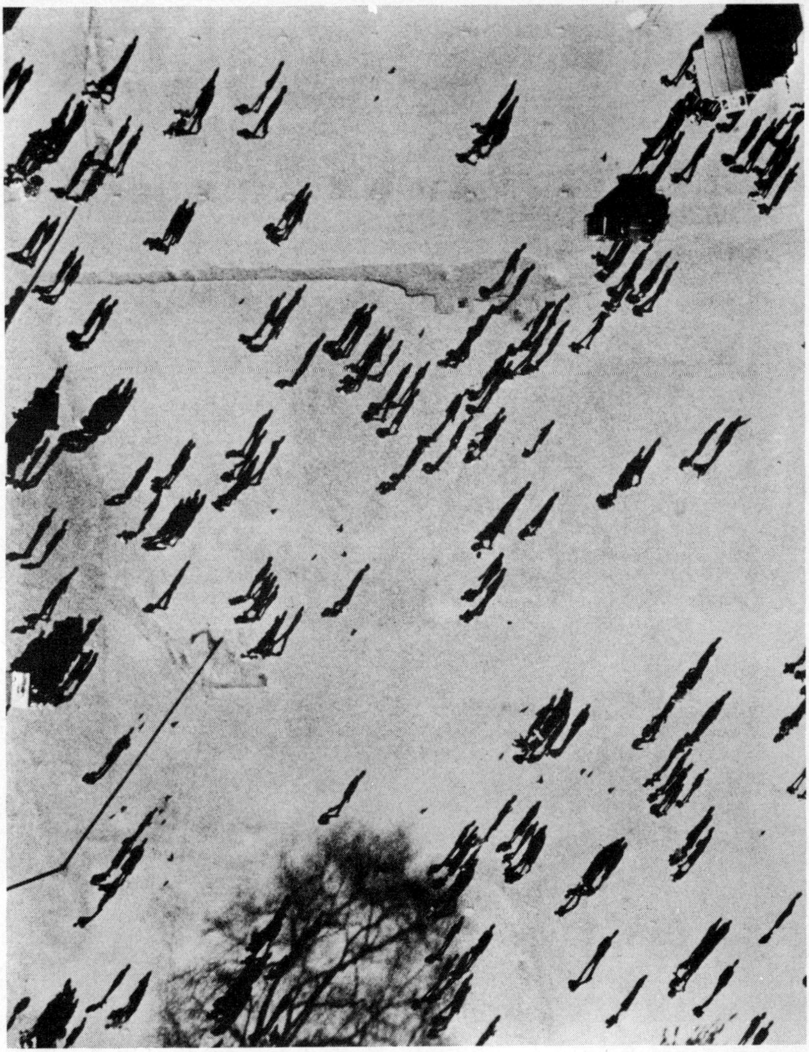

Fig. 28. *Le Joli Mai* (1963). Exuberance through light.

Fig. 29. *The Late Mattia Pascal* (1926). Morbidity through line and mass.

Courtesy of Contemporary Films

Fig. 30. *Sweet and Sour* (1963). Joy.

A superior film maker will recognize the types of undertones arising from the play of spaces, lines, and volumes on the screen and compose his shots in such a way that they reinforce rather than conflict with his theme, attitude, and intended mood. And since he is not a still photographer or a painter, the play of spaces in his composition must be dynamic rather than static (Fig. 31).

One director who succeeded brilliantly in exploiting this kind of compositional movement for achieving unique tonal effects was Ernst Lubitsch. The famous "Lubitsch touch"—characterized by a light, witty, sophisticated approach to a comedy of manners—depended in large part on Lubitsch's insistence on clearing his sets of bric-a-brac so that his camera could glide through space to give a sense of smoothness and ease. Often he welded gracefulness to lightness and airiness by having both character and camera etch out a line that was both vertical and circular: movement in a wide curve through a great volume of space (a tracking shot of Herbert Marshall's stand-in gliding up and down the wide arc of the stairs in *Trouble in Paradise*, 1932) or movement up into a spiral (craning the camera to pursue a department store employee moving up a spiral stairway in *Bluebeard's Eighth Wife*).

A few directors have been intensely conscious of the limits of size and shape of the screen itself in relation to volume and space to render tonal effects. As Arthur Knight points out, even in the early days of film making directors felt that "the wealth of visual imagery that they

Courtesy of the Museum of Modern Art

Fig. 31. *City Lights* (1931). A shift from the pathetic to the comic by means of facial movements and the adjustment of a cane.

were able to project made [the screen's] fixed and static dimensions seem quite inadequate," and eventually some of the more imaginative film makers, led by Griffith, "began to improvise ways of relating the shape of their screen to the mood, the action, the atmosphere of a shot, a sequence, or a scene."[8] Griffith himself achieved this by masking the lighted areas of the screen in various ways, either at top or bottom, and varied its size and shape to intensify the effect. As Knight notes, both limits to the spectrum of possibilities of this device are explored by Griffith in *Intolerance* within a matter of seconds:

To accentuate the far-flung hordes of Syrian warriors riding toward Babylon, for instance, he blacked out the top and bottom of the frame, producing a narrow, elongated frieze effect—strikingly similar to today's Cinemascope screen. But a moment later, when he wanted to emphasize the height of the walls of Babylon, he masked off the sides of the frame and showed the body of a single soldier hurtling down from the top of the ramparts in a vertical shaft of light.[9]

Cinema-Scope, together with all the other wide-screen variants, of course merely increased the possibilities for space play in a horizontal direction while ignoring any proportional requirements for vertical distance. As far back as the thirties Eisenstein protested against this "mechanical" and "passive" lateral extension of space without any thought to the dramatic and mood requirements for a strong vertical line, and he argued that if a practical means could not be devised for fluctuating the size and shape of the screen during projection, the best compromise was a square screen, since only this would allow comparable dramatic effects from the vertical and horizontal lines. Today directors of wide-screen productions are often forced to regard the increased lateral space in the same way that Victorian theatrical directors regarded their mammoth stages: not as space to be used dramatically and dynamically, but as a static space to be filled and cluttered with more objects and décor.

Obviously the best use that can be made of a disproportionate increase of width is in the historical epic, the travelogue with panoramic views, and the musical spectacular. But even these occasionally require a varying mood of intimacy or dramatic stress of detail, which can be conveyed only within a smaller space or by emphasis of vertical line or mass. At best one can recall only *parts* of wide-screen productions in which tone or mood is made more effective by the increased lateral vision. This occurs, of course, either when a strong horizontal line is needed for dramatic purposes, or when huge lateral spaces are needed to set off the minuteness or isolation of an object. A powerful illustration of the former is the almost unending line of savages rising over the top of a hill in *Zulu* (1964). A good example of a sense of isolation achieved by lateral space would be the shot of the small town in the middle of the desert in *Bad Day at Black Rock* (1954). In *Lawrence of Arabia* (1962) the way in which a black speck develops into a rider approaching on horseback is made more mystifying by the large surrounding areas of desert.

In achieving and maintaining continuity, the film maker adjusts settings and actors, or even photographic reality itself, in order to convey either his own attitude or that of his characters. His means are moving cameras, chemical processes, shifting camera angles, shot beginnings and endings, slow or accelerated motion, focal lengths, and space play. Using film he can be direct or ironical, simple or subtle, bitter about life or opportunistic (giving the public what it wants). He can win our admiration or our scorn. He cannot, however, hide what he is. As an artist good or bad, he tells us how he feels and what he thinks by the photographic reality he shows us and by the ways he manipulates it.

CHAPTER SEVEN

Theme

Just as a film maker cannot hide how he feels, he can disguise, but not hide, his meaning. In every stage of composition, the film maker arranging continuities through picture and sound is being guided by some one idea that gives unity to his film. Toward the effective presentation of his theme all matters of rhythm, imagery, and tone are techniques, but, as in poetry, what one says is intimately tied up with the way one says it. As the tone of voice may qualify the literal meaning of a sentence, a film maker's tempo, his images, and his point of view will modify the theme. Both *High Noon* (1952) and run-of-the-mill westerns may be about heroic sheriffs who withstand evil men, but the manner of presentation separates the adult western from one ridden with clichés.

The film maker's desire to present significant and complex thoughts through the cinematic methods at his command is often frustrated by the nonintellectual demands of his public. Certain popular movie genres like the western, the police-detective story, the spy drama, the war epic, the newspaper-crime thriller, the biography of a famous person, the sports story, the science fiction piece, the monster horror drama, and the jungle adventure appeal to audiences solely because of the intrigue, melodrama, and suspense generated by their plots and settings. Because of formula-like repetitions of character traits and story conflicts, each of these genres has become burdened with sets of stock characters and trite, predictable story lines. How often have we been exposed to the squabbling "sob sister" and crime reporter who beneath their fierce competition really love each other; or to the suave gambling casino owner whose gang of rustlers is broken up by the new marshal; or to the young composer-pianist who tries to choose between love and his career; or to

127

the honest boxer who turns down the bribe to "take a dive" and wins honestly against all odds; or to the mad scientist who wants to rule the world; or to the monster (prehistoric or extraterrestrial) that can only be destroyed by electricity or nuclear weapons; or to the secret agent who discovers that the master spy is the head of army intelligence? To be sure, the most entertaining of these B-films exploit all the cinematic techniques of camera movement and editing which Griffith had begun to perfect, and use all the technical advances that Hollywood has introduced since. But even the more elaborate of these—like the James Bond series—become tedious and ephemeral despite the frenzied acceleration of pace, the piling on of more gimmicky props (usually advanced-design instruments of torture and destruction) and added convolutions of plot.

The creators of these movies have made works that have ideological value only as the object of study of the fads and sociology of a particular time. Film, like any other art of mass appeal, is both a lamp and a mirror. Not only does it light the way to new fashions and mores, but it reflects (sometimes in a reverse image) what society at a given moment is. The showing on television of Hollywood films of the thirties and forties and revivals in art houses of dramatic films like those of Bogart and musicals like those of Busby Berkeley give us a retrospective notion of the manners and mores of those decades.

Most frequently the kinds of pressures which films unconsciously mirror are economic. In the early thirties, when the effects of the Depression were most abrasive, traditional genres underwent certain transformations. In films like *Dust Be My Destiny* (1939) the western hero becomes a tramp searching for a livelihood. But the obverse images of affluence are just as revealing. To offer escape from such direct realistic views of deprivation shown in films like *Dust Be My Destiny* and *The Grapes of Wrath* (1940) film makers like De Mille offered exotic historical spectacles teeming with every kind of material luxury; others transformed them into equally opulent musical comedies or farces of contemporary high life. The films of Busby Berkeley and of Ernst Lubitsch and those starring Fred Astaire and Ginger Rogers as well as a host of others known as "white telephone films" were, with their palatial settings, just as symptomatic of the Depression as the popular paper-money game known as Monopoly. A Berkeley-influenced musical, *Mad About Money*, made in England in 1936, even went so far as to have each chorus girl in one of its numbers dressed as a silver dollar.

Certain film makers, not content to be the unindividualized voices of their times, sought to impose a personal view and ideology upon their work. Often their cinematic efforts were more significant than their themes. Praised for the full shot, the close-up, night photography, the intercut, the iris, and cutting for tempo, suspense, and screen continuity, Griffith drew pragmatically from what had actually been used by others, but in his case in order to see inside and to find the moral significance of the thing observed.

Although Griffith allegorizes the world through technique and *mise en scène*, thematically all is not well in his films if they are considered as artistic organisms. There is, of course, a unity of theme and manner that enables one to speak of a Griffith style and a Griffith treatment. The one-reel *Drunkard's Reformation* of 1907 and *The Struggle* of 1931, about the effects of alcohol, or *A Corner in Wheat* of 1911 and *Isn't Life Wonderful?* of 1924, about the effects of inflation, continue to state the same moral and social problems with a new sophistication. The young heroine, needed at first for her photogenic complexion, continues her role of ingenue into the jazz age, until she becomes deceived (*Way Down East*) and rebellious (*True Heart Susie,* 1919). A man of few but firm ideas, Griffith, like other American naturalists, follows Darwin. The social-Darwinian idea that those best adapted to their environment are able to survive and the least adaptable are overcome finds comic expression in *Man's Genesis* (1912) and melodramatic expression in *The Musketeers of Pig Alley* (1912); social Darwinism also provides the basis for the effects of the strike in the modern story of *Intolerance,* released separately as *The Mother and the Law* (1919). Griffith's villains are not only mulattoes, half-breeds, rustlers, or "musketeer"-gangsters, but also retired virgins ("When women cease to attract men, they often turn to reform as a second choice"—a title from *Intolerance* that precedes a brothel raid) and bureaucrats (the draft-dodging sequence of four shots in *The Girl Who Stayed at Home,* showing a bribe going through four offices from a small town to Washington, D.C.).

The canon of Griffith's films reveals an *auteur* whose character and prejudices we know. He is a man capable of flag-waving and outrage, quick to violence, loquacious, egotistical (or inner-directed), both humanitarian and bigot. He is against the mean-minded rich and the shiftless poor; once overtaken by an idea, he is stubborn in maintaining its truth after it has been abandoned. In short, he is a Southerner such as described by Wilbur C. Cash in *The Mind of the South* and sometimes played on the screen by Randolph Scott. Conservative and yet liberal, reactionary and radical, tradition-bound yet open to change, manly yet sentimental, he seems, in the long run, to matter little as a man of thought. With equal fervor he could argue the supremacy of the white race and make pleas for toleration. He interpreted the Civil War as a joint victory of North and South as saviors of white Anglo-Saxon civilization: Seymour Stern rightly stresses the theme of *Birth* to lie in the intertitle, "The former enemies of North and South are united again in common defense of their common heritage";[1] furthermore, the prologue begins the Civil War drama with the arrival of Negro slaves from Africa and its second half is concerned with the Klan victory. Yet in *Intolerance* he could argue with four complex, intercut narratives against a force that never gets defined—the intolerance of Pharisees, of Catholics in Huguenot France, of Nebuchadnezzar, and of social workers—in a thematic mishmash. In *Broken Blossoms* he portrays the tragic struggles of a refined Chinese to acquire a blonde sweetheart against the intolerance of her drunken father.

All the while the spectator is enjoying momentary delights in what he sees on the Griffith screen, he is moved to question the value of the thought. Griffith can end one sequence with the death of an illegitimate baby and begin a second with a character named Hi Toller laying an egg, a tragic and comic juxtaposition of materials that gives delight. Yet the whole of *Way Down East,* a story that like a Shakespearean comedy ends with three marriages, remains trivial in conception.

More effective than Griffith in using cinematic techniques to convey significant meaning are film comedians of the early American cinema —Chaplin, Sennett, Laurel and Hardy, Keaton—who expressed directly, but most probably without conscious philosophic awareness, their satires, parodies, and burlesques of modern society. Sennett's accelerated shots of the inept chases conducted by his Keystone Kops highlight human fallibility in law and order. Frequently in the work of the Marx Brothers and sometimes in the films of Laurel and Hardy we can sense thematic statements about upper-class mores. When Margaret Dumont retains her ladylike dignity throughout the outrages perpetrated on her by the Marx Brothers, all the vanity in the *"grande dame"* pose of rich ladies is satirically exposed. In Laurel and Hardy's *Wrong Again* (1928) Hardy initiates a sight gag—performed with a twist of the open hand—to indicate that rich people like everything "ass backwards." Reinforced by the pair's mistake in mending a statue with buttocks reversed, this gesture grows into an overwhelming spoof of upper-class values.

As ingenuous social critics Laurel and Hardy were always directing their barbs upward from the lower rung of the social ladder. Usually shown as members of the working class (carpenters, icemen, piano movers, toymakers), they are content to remain so. Their humorous collision with middle- and upper-class society is not born of a desire to crash into it, or even to crush it, but to serve it more efficiently. Harold Lloyd, on the other hand, mostly derives his humor by portraying the earnest, success-minded young man seeking his way into an "in-group." In *The Freshman* (1925) Lloyd's approach to life can be characterized, as one critic put it, as that of "a 'George Babbitt' . . . [who] fills himself with secret slogans, formulas and rituals for 'getting off on the right foot,' and for 'making a go of it' . . . [and who] is so serious about his social goal, he is too involved in life around him to achieve any social distance."[2] It is interesting to note that although the physical act of climbing is prevalent in both Laurel and Hardy skits and in Harold Lloyd features as a metaphor for social advancement, it has quite a different meaning: Ollie's attempts to get Stanley to boost him up lamp posts, walls, and stairs have no other aim than pride in a job well done, whereas Harold's hair-raising escapades on the sides of tall buildings are either by-products of some self-promoting scheme or a bid for heroic acclaim.

From these comedies of manners, based on the collision of either ethos or class (Fig. 32), it is but a short step to the cinema of the absurd with its heroes neither representing a class nor caring much about class values but blithely operating entirely upon some principle of internal logic which often seems like chaos and mayhem. From the most frenetic antics of the Marx Brothers, Chaplin, and Jerry Lewis to the more restrained movements of W. C. Fields, Keaton, and Jacques Tati, we are involved in an eccentric world composed of only the bits and fragments of recognizable logic. It is, in fact, from this special cinema world that much of the intellectually respectable "theater of the absurd" has drawn its inspiration. Witness, for instance, Ionesco's testimonial that the three greatest influences on his work were Groucho, Chico, and Harpo Marx (Fig. 33). Ionesco's landscape, in which matter proliferates in a geometrical progression (the constant carrying in of chairs in *The Chairs* or the crowding of furniture into the small room in *The New Tenant*, for example), is part of the same *Duck Soup* (1933) carnival in which Groucho buys from Chico an armful of books, each one a key to another, to find out the name of a single race horse; or in which an endless parade of people streams into a tiny ship's cabin (*A Night at the Opera*, 1935). And Ionesco's *reductio ad absurdum* of the syntactical structure of language—as a shock to cliché-ridden middle-class thought—has its parallels not only in Groucho's and Chico's puns but in Chaplin's and

Fig. 32. *My Little Chickadee* (1940). Frontier *commedia dell'arte*.

Tati's deflation of language itself, as in the blurred speech of the politician in *City Lights* and the incomprehensible public address system in *Mr. Hulot's Holiday*.

When a director's ideological concern becomes so strong that it becomes a constant, burning passion, and when that passion is in turn served by artistic genius, the result can be a great—albeit didactic—work of art. Driven by his enthusiasm for the proletarian uprisings in Russia, Eisenstein created in *Strike* a masterpiece of cinematic art despite its moments of crudely handled, though humorous, bias, as for example when the faces of the capitalist spies dissolve into the faces of animals. The intended "message," as well as the plot line itself, is inextricably bound up with his joyful experiments with the medium. In setting up powerful visual metaphors, like the cross-cutting of the slaughter of a bull with the massacre of a mob, and the pattern of images which establish the motif of spying (close-ups of eyes, an optometrist's sign depicting spectacles, the unusual ocular effect of a pile of discarded train wheels),

Courtesy of Universal Pictures

Fig. 33. *Horse Feathers* (1932). The three greatest influences on the Theater of the Absurd.

Eisenstein creates an imagistic poem for his socialistic lesson and for evoking our sympathy for the downtrodden mob.

Similarly Leni Riefenstahl's initially sincere attempts to realize Hitler's dream of recording the 1936 Berlin Olympics in such a way as to reveal the ideals of Nazism gave way to a true artist's desire to render the events in as poetic and dramatic a way as possible. Luckily the Nazi slogan which she was to demonstrate—"Strength, Grace and Endurance"—was both general enough to be acceptable to any people or social system embodying classical ideals and was, like Beauty and Truth, the logical goal to which any humanistic artist would aspire in his work. Actually the closest the film, *Olympia*, comes to reminding us of Nazism is in the insinuations of Aryan superiority, as when the blond torchbearer arrives in Berlin with the Olympic flame, or the few glimpses of Hitler in the stands.

With unlimited freedom to set up elaborate camera installations (in pits, on running boards of cars, in balloons, and so on, both inside and outside the stadium) and to expose as much film as she wished, Riefenstahl for two years edited and re-edited her footage until she produced neither a document nor a doctrine but a unified paean to human aspiration based on events restructured in time and space, suffused with the lyricism of arranged light and movement, and charged with dramatic tensions enhanced by the cutting. A sequence which opens quite conventionally with a succession of male athletes diving into a pool shifts into an almost surrealistic aerial ballet as the camera switches into slow motion and into various unusual angles so that bodies seem to be floating freely through space, especially when photographed from below against the darkening sky. These are finally superimposed in composite shots accompanied by stirring music. It is as if the whole performance is mysteriously transferred from the element of water to the element of air, from the time-bound mundane to the celestially eternal. In more quiet moods she captures a more intimate lyricism of movement when the camera, tracking an exercising runner at extreme proximity, shows the play of facial and chest muscles, juxtaposed with the shadow of the entire body on the road and the flickering of light and foliage in the background. The contrary mood—excitement from the competitions themselves—is given a greater epic sweep and elevation in Part I by shots of the Olympic flame burning high above the stadium, often into the night, and in Part II by occasional shots of the flags of the winning countries being hoisted on high.

Unimpeded by story line or even by an obligation to be conventionally reportorial, Riefenstahl was free to construct her grand mosaic in the editing room with complete artistic absorption. She insists always that human aspiration defies physical laws. Luckily events had conspired to keep her propagandistic concerns to a minimum: not only had Germany failed to win many of the competitions but Hitler had stormed out of the stadium early in the contests. Her work was therefore left unaffected by any obligation to be deeply chauvinistic, unlike her involvement in *Triumph of the Will* (1936), which suffers from a mechanized staginess.

Semiofficial propagandists like Eisenstein and Riefenstahl, who aspire to be artists as well, continually operate in a kind of double jeopardy. To the extent that they wish to transcend their imposed themes by exercising creative imagination, they run the risk of irritating the authorities by subordinating the message to experimentation or by attempting to disguise their propaganda with an empty artistic formalism

or displays of film technique. Both Riefenstahl and Eisenstein occasionally came dangerously close to self-conscious assertions of an irrelevant
technical virtuosity. As delightful as the cream separator sequence in
The Old and New (1929) is, it becomes an abstraction of light and
motion severed from any connection with agricultural collectivism. Later
on in the film Eisenstein, in a burst of humor, drops all pretense of involvement with his Marxist theme by momentarily turning his collective
farm into a parody of the Hollywood western. The tractor operator leaps
onto his driver's seat—in a series of overlap shots designed to prolong
the action—like a cowboy hero mounting his horse (Fig. 34); and on

Courtesy of the Museum of Modern Art

Fig. 34. *Old and New* (*Staroie i Novoie*) (1929). Ride 'em, cowboy.

the string of carts tied to the tractor a peasant leaps from wagon to
wagon in an obvious lampoon of the traditional chase across the tops of
boxcars in train robbery scenes. His theme, like Riefenstahl's, insists that
what is human surpasses what is doctrinal.

There is no question that the art of film has matured to the degree
that we may now claim to have a "cinema of ideas," something akin to

the "theater of ideas" developed by Ibsen and Shaw almost a century ago. Herman Weinberg recognized this as early as 1938 when he commended the "social reality" of American directors like Griffith, Vidor, Milestone, Leroy, Ford, Chaplin, Capra, Lang, and von Stroheim. Citing Vidor as "our foremost commentator on the American scene," he praised *The Big Parade* (1925) for breaking with "the then popular Hollywood sport of treating war as a comedy of doughboys and ma'mselles," *Our Daily Bread* (1934) for its realistic treatment of the problems of communal farmers, and *The Citadel* (1938) for being "almost a plea for socialized medicine."[3]

While some of these directors became great social critics because of a direct representation of their serious concern (LeRoy in *I Am a Fugitive from a Chain Gang* [1932], Lang in *Fury* [1936], Ford in *The Informer* [1935], and Lubitsch in *The Man I Killed* [1932]), at least one—Charlie Chaplin—became a powerful scourge through the more oblique means of what Weinberg calls "Hogarthian humor." In *Modern Times*, "the darkest and most troubled of all his films, despite its gargantuan hilarity," Chaplin dared, Weinberg reminds us, "to make comedy around things of terrible veracity—strikes, unemployment, police versus workers, street demonstrations, the 'speed-up,' and the whole part and parcel of the capitalist system."[4] However, just as Max Beerbohm in 1906 found Ibsen to be not so much a conscious reformer as rather like a volcano erupting because of some inner fury, so also did Weinberg in 1938 see most of these film makers as deriving the "lifeblood" of their criticism from "their capacity to be angry" rather than from any studied motive to ameliorate human nature or society:

> None of these men, save perhaps Griffith, was a crusader; none began with any particular credo, social or political theory, nor was any moved by a consistent inner urge to look at life square in the eye and do something about it, save, perhaps, von Stroheim.[5]

Today this social-philosophic tendency in film makers has become more conscious and pointed. The detective-story films of Akira Kurosawa, for instance, have as their model neither the intruder into nice families nor the syndicate of criminals, as do American counterparts in the genre. In *Stray Dog* (1949) and *High and Low* (1963) the apparent subject is the art of detection, as in Sherlock Holmes stories, but the real subject is unmotivated goodness, like Bogart's in *The Maltese Falcon*. Both Kurosawa films are morally instructive.

In *Stray Dog* Kurosawa's detective, played by Toshiro Mifune, is a good man who *wills* himself to do good. The film begins with a shot of a mongrel breathing hard, but the sound track produces not the dog's sounds, but the rumbling of a train in motion. Since the chief setting is the railroad and the secondary character a "stray" veteran of World War II, the train's rumbling and the dog's breathing introduce both the film's setting and its chief symbol. The protagonist, also a veteran, has become a detective. While he is riding the train in the rush hour, his gun is stolen. The detective is ready to resign from the force. With the help of older men on the force, he learns two lessons of life: first, that the "stray dog" who has stolen his gun is likely to become a "mad dog," desperate enough to kill many; and, second, that his own ill fortune may be turned into good fortune.

That the stray dog becomes a mad dog is only one element of the parable. Like the detective-hero, the gun robber has been struggling for existence in postwar Japan, both men having had their knapsacks stolen on their return to Japan. The stray dog has hardened into evil. In the end, Satan-like, he becomes a creature of despair, causing evil out of his will-less inability to do good. The detective, however, persists in good. In their final confrontation, the two grapple amid flowers (a garden of Eden) in a Miltonic struggle between good and evil, which, according to Milton, "first came into the world as twin progeny." Donald Richie, in *The Japanese Film*, says of this struggle that the two are indistinguishable—good and evil being covered by a primeval ooze.[6] Unfortunately, he does not take the outcome of the struggle into consideration. When both men become exhausted, the detective handcuffs the gun robber. Their similarity is only momentary. The good detective triumphs by an act of will. The message, therefore, is that good Japanese can overcome the hardships in their social lives by a will to do good.

A second lesson of *Stray Dog* applies both to the Japanese of 1949 and to men generally. The detective who wants to resign in the face of the loss of his gun at first accepts despair. When he subsequently engages in the struggle for his honor, he performs the difficult task of making fortune reverse itself. By stalking a woman who knows where the gun is, by following the guns-for-hire criminal syndicate who lend out his gun, and by, at length, fulfilling his plan of finding and bringing to justice the original gun robber, the hero brings about the capture of a ring of criminals, not of his own enemy alone. The message for the Japanese of 1949 is that they too may force their destiny—a philosophy that is the opposite of fatalism. It is a message that absorbs best what Americans pretended to teach the Japanese in their occupation of that country. Armed with a philosophy of good works, men may turn bad fortune into good fortune.

Fourteen years later, in *High and Low*, Kurosawa restates his theme of the triumph of good over evil in a second detective-story parable. Based on *King's Ransom*, an American detective novel of the Eighty-seventh Precinct series by Ed McBain (pseudonym of Evan Hunter, who wrote *The Blackboard Jungle* and *A Summer House*), this Tohoscope (Cinema-Scope) film uses various devices that raise the film above the level of the melodrama and the sentimentality toward which the genre is prone.

In Kurosawa's adaptation, an intern tries to kidnap the son of a shoe manufacturer but demands the same thirty-million-yen ransom for the chauffeur's son whom he has taken by mistake. For the first hour of the film, Kurosawa restricts the setting to the rich man's house on a hill in Yokohama, the "High" of the title. In order to gain control of National Shoes, the self-made capitalist has mortgaged his possessions. His noble purpose is not naked power, but rather the God-like role of controlling what base capitalists would pervert: he rejects their planned obsolescence for increased shoe consumption. After the kidnaping, the executive, faced with the alternative of saving the chauffeur's boy or maintaining his money and his social position, chooses the former course. The setting then moves to the pay-off, to the boy's return, and to the kidnaper, who represents the "Low" of the title.

After the pay-off, the police, who have been docile, undertake the recovery in the mass police action common to such films. "Now," says the lovable bull-like detective, "let us become bloodhounds." When the police wander in the slum valley below the house on the hill, one of them, looking up, says, "The kidnaper is right. That house makes me sore." Kurosawa shows the house on the hill, cuts to the cramped, ugly houses in the valley beside a stream in which the hill house is reflected, plays on the sound track Schubert's "The Trout," and leads us along with the kidnaper to his room.

The story is not new and the genre is low-brow, but Kurosawa's elevation of the theme is strong. The kidnaper is not made psychopathic. Instead, like Dostoevsky's Raskolnikov, he is smitten with *Angst*, the despair, partly social, that comes when one finds that life is hell. Satan-like, the kidnaper has set out to make a fortunate man unfortunate. After receiving a death sentence, the kidnaper requests to see not a priest but the good man whom he has undertaken to torment. In a confrontation of good and evil, high and low, the tycoon asks, "Why must you hate?"

In torment, the kidnaper trembles, weeps, and shakes furiously. He explains that from the Hell below, the house on the hill looked like Heaven. In a final image, an iron curtain falls between them: good on one side, evil on the other—the inescapable duality of choice that confronts each man.

Like other Christian artists, Kurosawa sees the triumph of unity and therefore of good and of God in the moral war among men. He tells in detective-story form a parable of the ultimate as well as the daily triumph of good over evil. The victory is hard fought and far from hollow. Kurosawa's good man does not grow tired. Vigilant in his goodness, he struggles for his triumph.

The screen pullulates with small delights that enhance his theme. After the pay-off, when two cases containing ransom money are shoved through a seven-inch opening in the train's bathroom window, the tycoon washes his hands as if after defecation. The moral evil has made him feel his body to be dirty. At the capture, a radio ironically plays "good night" music, the song being "There's No Tomorrow." In another bit of sound montage, Kurosawa creates cosmic implications for his parable. He uses three electronic beeps as he shows a panorama of Yokohama—sounds that function in the film like Chekhov's famous "sound of a harp string breaking," a cosmic omen in *The Cherry Orchard*.

While Fellini, Antonioni, and Bergman—Kurosawa's compeers—demand only a hesitant faith in right action, Kurosawa insists on the simple duality of good and evil. For example, Bergman's Christian trilogy is more complex. The *Angst* of the tired good before an uncomprehending God leaves the good with only the forms of worship: doubting parsons preach on. Kurosawa's parables show men the joy of goodness that controls fortune. In times of simpler folk, Jesus spoke in terms of sheepherders and fishermen about how men should live. Basing his films on the more complex imagery of modern subcultural fiction, Kurosawa uses the detective story to urge democracy and to restate a Dostoevskian faith in man.

Among the works of recent film artists one finds a cinema of social and cultural awareness comparable to the literature that gave us *The Waste Land*. The difficulty in enjoying Antonioni's films does not lie in their lack of story, any more than it does in Chekhov's plays. Their allegedly slow movement and the argument that Antonioni presents character in virtually plotless films proceed from a misunderstanding of method.

The usual film drama has a beginning (we are introduced to a character in a situation), a middle (the character in conflict reaches a point where he is either changed by or changes his environment), and an ending (the conflict is resolved and the characterization concluded). Generally in films where the story element predominates, the best presentation gives primary emphasis to the character, his dilemma along with incidents that convey it, and his resolution of that dilemma. In Robert Mulligan's *Baby the Rain Must Fall* (1965), based on Horton Foote's play *The Traveling Lady*, the protagonist reveals his inability to adjust to society: a prisoner on parole, an ex-drunk, a husband and father who has been unable to care for his family, he lacks the eloquence to confess his love-hate for a lady who has reared him. His emotional outlet is rock 'n' roll singing. Willing to deny himself this outlet and to study in night school in order to please his foster mother, he is freed, he thinks, from this obligation by her death, only to discover that the sheriff will carry out her will. In the end he tries to attack the buried woman and is returned to jail, leaving his wife and child alone to travel on to another town.

We have chosen to tell the story of *Baby the Rain Must Fall* because it has the characteristics of the existentialist film that Antonioni has mastered. The hero has vague motivation for his actions, his foster mother none, yet the *Angst* of a man who wants to "break out," who remains tense in calm small-town surroundings, is conveyed by bleak images of the American prairie—somewhat dusty, largely treeless, adorned with antiquated, sprawling houses or with shacks. In the best sequence, the sound track carries the maudlin lyrics of the title song and the hero plants a small tree while wife and child look on in joy at a family life that will be short-lived. Furthermore, the story is told directly, with images, as of the small tree, merely complementing the story with a mood of loneliness. That mood is secondary to the story of the traveling lady and her spouse, conveyed with an emphasis on incidents, as in conventional literature.

In *Red Desert* (1965) Antonioni also tells a story, but by indirection. Images, as in T. S. Eliot's *The Waste Land*, carry the burden of communication. In such communication, the eye and the ear perceive the *materia prima* from which the spectator will draw conclusions about plot and character. By repetition of form and color, by a focus trick, by dual-purpose action, and by sound montage, the story of a woman coming to terms with her fears will be conveyed. *Red Desert* is a highly organized film, every detail in a state of becoming, i.e., moving toward meaning. Only at the end does the significance of visual and aural patterns emerge. Then the spectator realizes that he has been partaking, with Antonioni, of an experience and that the fragments observed have a single unified action as their goal.

An analogy to modern poetry clarifies Antonioni's *modus operandi*. In *The Waste Land*, the fragments of verse from "April is the cruellest month . . . mixing memory and desire" to "*Shantih shantih shantih*" are coordinated into an experience of desolation that prepares one for hope. As the reader moves from image to image, gathering allusions and following anecdotes, such as those in Part II, "A Game of Chess," he discovers that image, allusion, and anecdote have been constellated to support the chief image, that of the title and its overtones of a fertility rite. Each image of Eliot's poem resolves itself into futility, anxiety, fear, *accedium* (spiritual despair). Marie, who must hold on tight as she toboggans down a slope; the high-born lady who fears the sounds that prove to be the wind under the door; Lil, who aborts after having five already; the typist who after being seduced puts a record on the gramophone; the condoms ("other remembrances of summer nights") that are part of the flotsam on the Thames where swans glided and Elizabeth and Leicester once rode—all these images of fear and disgust evoke, rather than state, the theme.

The opening color of *Red Desert* is gray, like that of black-and-white films. Immediately, as names in color are written on the screen, the color film becomes evident. The background behind the craftsmen's names is out of focus. The immediate impression is that Antonioni does not want the pictures to interfere with names of director, script girl, and the like. Such is not the case.

After these out-of-focus shots of a Ravenna chemical factory during which the titles unroll, accompanied by an electronic score of a soprano voice, Antonioni reveals, in close shot, puffs of yellow flame that spring rhythmically from a smokestack. When the heroine buys a sandwich from a worker who has already started to eat it, she retires to a wooded area. While she eats it, the yellow flame, now in the background behind her, continues to be ejected rhythmically. The yellow fire puff is not merely the repetition of a detail, nor does it merely establish place. Taken in conjunction with other details, the yellow fire will emerge as the unifying symbol of the film.

The smokestack, along with the factory, the home, the shop the heroine is preparing, the canal amid shacks and rubbish heaps—all these details not only provide settings but also show the sludge and the geometric order of the modern wasteland, the impersonal "desert" that contrasts with the heroine's internal disorder. As existential woman, she is trying to come to terms with a mechanistic world, in itself neither good nor evil and, as Antonioni shows it, something beautiful. In a *Cahiers* interview, Antonioni told Jean-Luc Godard that a row of new concrete-and-steel buildings is as beautiful as a row of trees, perhaps even more beautiful because men are less accustomed to it. The settings are, nevertheless, carefully chosen for bareness, and much of the weather is misty. Antonioni does not show the heroine and her child in a crowded, sunny park, although she probably takes him there, just as T. S. Eliot does not violate his art by a happy recollection of a calm day at the beach or of an evening dance, although he loved dancing. Giuliana (Monica Vitti) is trying to adjust in a particular world that the settings symbolize.

The chief means that Antonioni uses to show the world as it appears to Giuliana is the out-of-focus shot. At the beginning, therefore, as and when the titles unroll, the Ravenna factory is out of focus, seen, although we do not know it then, from her point of view. When Giuliana observes the strikers at the factory, they too are out of focus, although when Monica Vitti enters the out-of-focus frame her back is shown in focus. Whenever Giuliana is among people or things that frighten her and with which she is trying to come to terms, the focus is off. At one point in the film, a shot of five persons lounging on a bed in a shack begins out of focus. Just when it seems that the theater projectionist has made an error, the back of Monica Vitti's head, completely in focus, again enters the frame: what the spectator is seeing is the loungers as they appear to Giuliana. Objective reality, as Antonioni sees it, is in focus. Precise also are pictures of husband, son, home, and those objects with which Giuliana is familiar and for which she feels some love.

Through a set of incidents, Giuliana tries to come to terms with the world. Finding herself filled with fears, induced in antecedent actions (an automobile accident from which, however, she has recovered and an attempted suicide) Giuliana, wife of Ugo, a chemical engineer, and mother of Valerio, comes with her son to his factory, meets Corrado, meets Corrado again when she is at the shop she is planning in order to distract herself, visits shacks with her husband, finds herself getting worse—more of the world she knows discomforting her—nurses her son when she fears he has polio, goes to Corrado's hotel room when her husband is off on business to London, and visits the factory with her son once again at the end of the film. The story of *The Red Desert* (*Il deserto rosso*)—a particular reference to Ravenna's environs—proceeds, therefore, by incidents, as does *Baby the Rain Must Fall* and other films in which the story is directly told. These incidents, however, subserve a profound emotion and pose a serious question: how in the face of private misery in a world that seems remote may a sensitive woman come to terms with family and land?

The answer lies in two moments near the end of the film that in technique draw upon the imagery evoked earlier. The first occurs during Valerio's illness, a "classically selfish masculine trick," as Bosley Crowther says of the feigned symptoms of polio.[7] In order to amuse the bedridden boy, Giuliana tells the story of a girl, obviously herself, who lived near the sea, like a Nereid; this story is shown in lucid pictures that contrast with the out-of-focus shots of Giuliana's present reality, the girl swimming in a cove, perceiving an empty ship, and hearing the electronically recorded soprano voice. The story shows the idealized world of Giuliana's youth. Her description of the "rocks like flesh" means that the nature surrounding her was somewhat animate, as it was to the boy Wordsworth, a source of pleasure that she no longer feels in her disjunctive contacts. One answer lies in withdrawal from the present.

The second moment that provides an answer to how to live with despair reunites the final image and the first of the film. When Valerio asks his mother about the yellow smoke, now emerging from the smokestack in a steady relentless stream, Giuliana tells him that it is poisonous. When he asks further whether it kills the birds, she tells him that by this time the birds have learned to stay clear of the poisoned air.

Armed with the collected images and incidents, the spectator is enabled to discover after the fact what he has seen. One mystery has been the sandwich that Giuliana buys from a startled worker. Why, since she is well off and since her child, who accompanies her, is not hungry, does Giuliana make this purchase, running off to eat it? The answer appears to be that to her nervous eye, for which many other things have been out of focus, the sandwich, something familiar and therefore desirable, appeared, as it were, *in focus*; consequently, she sought to possess it and to devour it. (She says to Corrado later that she would eat him also if she loved him.) Another shot, one that states Giuliana's problem, involves the fog that rolls in between her and five persons from whom she is fleeing but who, nevertheless, represent the real world to which she is trying to remain attached. At the end of the film Giuliana is not greatly hopeful that the world will be in clearer focus or less fogbound. She merely has reached a point of knowing that she must avoid some things: incipient violence (as of the strikers), sex without love (as among the friends who chat about aphrodisiacs—a subject she likes), and cold human relations (as in her sexual affair with Corrado). The theme of *Red Desert*, made indirectly, is that a woman of feeling will continue to find much that will puzzle and frighten her. There is no easy solution, but as in Samuel Beckett's *The unnamable*, one must go on, one can't go on, one goes on.

From the American film farces of Mack Sennett to the European cinema of ideas of today film makers have expressed, either consciously or unconsciously, their notions of how man ought and ought not to behave in society and the world. At last both the critics and the public are willing to admit that the film artist is as capable as the painter, the sculptor, the novelist, and the poet of stating the great themes of our time. For a sense of man's religious impotence one can go to see Buñuel's *The Exterminating Angel* (1962). For the meaning of *tedium vitae*, to Antonioni's *La Notte*, or for the joy of life to Visconti's *Rocco and His Brothers* (1960). Man's continual quest for God is perhaps more understandable after viewing Bergman's *The Seventh Seal* (1956), while man's search for himself may seem more unfathomably complex than ever after the experience of Fellini's 8½ and *Juliet of the Spirits* (1965). The best of these film makers, however, have made their vision such an intimate part of the cinematic means they have used to express it that it is ultimately impossible to talk about their themes without discussing the story, rhythm of composition, images, and tones that constitute the total architectural structure of their films.

CHAPTER EIGHT

The Film Art

THE art of the film is born out of the triumph over limitations in the medium. A filmstrip breaks, a photographer makes a double exposure, lighting lacks the proper intensity, lens settings create blurred or off-focus outlines, the film stock itself is of grainy texture or fogged, or the camera itself is so heavy as not to be movable toward or away from objects being filmed. These early hazards in recording reality led to the possibility of film art. That celluloid breaks is a hazard that evolved into the shot, the plastic building block out of which a whole film would be made: shots that end abruptly may be spliced together into coherent or poetic continuity or montage. That a camera jams, causing double exposure—a problem that still photographers hate when they have forgotten to advance the roll of film—led in cinematography to the dissolve, the fluid transition that connects images closely related in concept or time. Underexposure or overexposure and soft focus or off-focus enable film makers to distort for emotion, atmosphere, or symbolism the light and lines that define an object. Intentionally grainy effects in modern films, as in Truffaut's *Jules and Jim*, lend deliberate archaism to a story set in the early 1900's, when film stock lacked textural refinement. Calculated fogging of the film negative in the laboratory creates the fade, a device which, like the eye or the curtain in a theater, opens and closes a scene. As film makers needed to get closer to what they were filming, mobile cameras and specialized lenses enabled them to come to the mountain instead of always having to have the mountain of actors and objects come before them. The minds that recreate reality through film need refinements of cinematic machinery.

Since the natural accidents that befell film makers like Méliès gave them a larger scope in which to become artists, it is logical that film makers continue to "destroy" and distort the medium even further, in order to increase its potential for expression. Behaving sometimes like impressionist painters, at other times like action painters, experimental film makers capture mere glimpses and fragments of events by means of swish-panning, single-frame editing, and dual projections of different images on juxtaposed screens or on a single screen. They force the viewer's optic nerves into new ways of seeing. Still other experimenters abandon the technical conventions of both filming and projection, eliminating the need for a camera by pasting objects like moth wings upon clear filmstrips (Stan Brakhage in *Mothlight*, 1963) or eliminating the need for a screen by projecting the image upon the bodies of dancers in a discotheque. This last "happening" illustrates another way in which the film medium is being expanded, that is, simply by being combined with other art forms—dancing, live drama, spectaculars of light and sound, and electronic concerts—in performances known as "mixed media" entertainments.

Yet in restoring reality or even in conveying through new technique and mixed media his complex inner states, the film maker may or may not achieve art. Gertrude Stein tells of a fourth-rate painter who said to a first-rate painter, "No matter how you try to escape it, we are contemporaries." Although the first-rate film maker and the fourth-rate film maker capture through motion photography those raw materials of existence that provide continuity through a succession of pictorial accords and oppositions, the fourth-rate is likely to strive for originality and end with banality. The first-rate film maker keeps a film from going bad not only by self-discipline but also by authoritarian aesthetic control over those who work under him. By ruthless rejection of irrelevant and inferior contributions he maintains a standard of artistic excellence.

Various craftsmen must submit to his aesthetic authority. His task is to find the center of interest in the work of the cinematographer, the scriptwriter, the actor, and the set designer. He finds these moments by stressing a process shot at a particular time or by allowing the actor to emote. Sometimes he calls for a special sound effect, like the wail of an ambulance described earlier for *Young Man with a Horn*. He may find a blank screen effective or choose to show in close shot the dancing feet of Fred Astaire. Like the conductor of a symphony orchestra, he may urge into momentary prominence either a single contributor or a particular ensemble of contributors, forcing others to retire for the sake of the harmony he wishes to achieve.

The cinematographer or director of photography is especially adept in molding light and dark into reality and fantasy, as Lucien Ballard does in *The Lodger* (1944) when he illuminates moving faces surrounded by pitch blackness or figures grouped together in silhouette. Sometimes a lighting director will assist him, as when he brings light to Anna Karina's eyes in *My Life to Live* (Fig. 35). The cinematographer

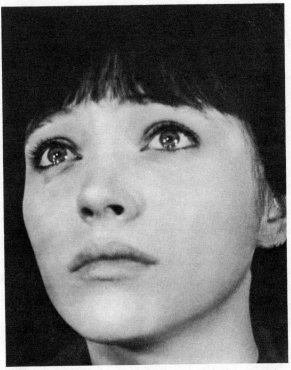

Courtesy of Contemporary Films

Fig. 35. *My Life to Live* (1962). Inner light from an outer source.

also may have an expert eye for framing the shot from the angle or distance that most effectively "composes" it. It is chiefly the job of the cinematographer to overcome with his technology and art the illusions of reality represented by such problems as the reverse turning of a wagon wheel, or the absence of a fixed point of reference for a moving plane or boat. Directors as formidable as Griffith, Welles, and Lang have carefully heeded the advice of their cinematographers.

The actor because of his popularity and fame, not to mention his artistic accomplishments, may seem at times to be controlling the direction and form a film takes. Yet a director can cut an actor's body into fragments by a series of close-ups in order that its significant details be contributions to the whole film. He may even, like Eisenstein, negate the need for professional actors in small roles by creating in the cutting room what is known as "typage acting," intercutting into a dramatic sequence photographs from the film library of faces with neutral expression that appear to be emotionally reacting to a dramatic situation. Once Bergman and Bresson find on the actor's face the decisive expression that sustains the mood of a sequence, they delete follow-up expressions so vivid on the stage: the result of their restraint in hewing to a single tone or theme is that actors in these classically controlled films often, as Sarris says, "have difficulty breathing in . . . rigid frame."[1]

Dreyer, on the other hand, courts ensemble acting by allowing a shot of two actors, say, to run for some time, preferring to pan from one to the other, or simply holding them in two-shot, rather than cutting their scene into many segments. Though he seems more generous toward actors, Dreyer also limits their range to make their work conform to his needs. Yet in the absence of a strong director, a performer may bring to a film excellence of timing and conviction, proving Elia Kazan's dictum that an actor must have the role he is portraying contained in his life. In successful films, the actor's contribution is no less essential than a director's in creating aesthetic harmony out of filmed reality, for a director cannot make art out of ineffectively acted sequences.

Even before the appearance of talkies the scriptwriter had an important role in the making of a film. He had to concoct a story line and perhaps compose the printed titles. But the director had always to subordinate these contributions to the visual continuity that he set out to achieve. Griffith enjoyed the screenplays submitted by Anita Loos enough to buy them, but he did not use them because their abundance of words made them uncinematic. When printed titles "telegraphed" the action that was about to be presented visually, as they did in She (1913), or when they burst out into poetic effusions, as did some of those composed by Griffith for his films, they allowed the scriptwriter to predominate in a way that was injurious to the film's visual continuity and impact.

During the early talkies, the scriptwriter sprang into greater prominence, especially when called upon to adapt or write the "photoplay," a rather literal recording of a stage drama. But even here actors' actions and reactions and the camera's ways of looking speak louder than words. The verbal wit provided Groucho Marx by S. J. Perelman is undeniably masterful and brilliant, but what would Groucho's puns be without Groucho's concomitant raised eyebrows, bobbing cigar, and slouching gait? A competent director like Leo McCarey knew how to energize visually the incessant verbal flow from Groucho and Chico by shifting from close-ups of facial expressions to middle shots of body movement, or to punctuate the scenes of dialogue with the silent antics of Harpo. Sometimes Groucho, mugging, would say, "Get this in close-up."

The degree to which the set designer contributes to the making of a film is dependent upon the atmosphere and setting chosen for it. If the film is shot almost entirely on location, then his work involves refining nature with artifice. But when much of the film is shot in the studio—in the case of the UFA directors all of it was—he had to use his ingenuity to fulfill the director's demands for authenticity in objects and background, viz., von Stroheim's demand for a complete wiring system in the replica of a hotel room or Welles' insistence on ceilings for the rooms to be encompassed by his low-angle shots in *Citizen Kane*. When the director wishes decor to participate in the film not as gratuitous detail but as image or idea, as when von Sternberg in *The Scarlet Empress* (1934) uses the formal lines of the carriage adjacent to furs, fruit, and flowers to highlight hedonism (Fig. 36), then the set designer's contribution to the director's art becomes paramount.

The tensions of all the craftsmen who have worked on a film come to a climax in the dubbing room when from the "rough cut" the completed film will be assembled. They have attended daily rushes after each day's shooting and have come together to see the final polishing of the gem. If they have not lost them already, the cinematographer may still lose his "best shots," the actor his "best scenes," the scriptwriter "his best lines," the *metteur en scène* his "best effects." The cinematographer may see carefully framed sequences distorted by the laboratory work or made insignificant by uninspired acting. The actor may complain that the music is drowning out his lines or sentimentalizing what he has tried to convey; he may prefer silence. The scriptwriter will see a set of visual continuities that sometimes underline his words or sometimes make his dialogue unnecessary. Nevertheless, each of the set designers, property men, costume designers, along with technical advisers, hairdressers, make-up men, stunt men, and other stand-ins—all who contribute to the

Courtesy of Universal Pictures

Fig. 36. *The Scarlet Empress* (1934). Decor.

mise en scène, workers on the tiles of the mosaic, find their work in the larger context of the whole film. Even the "grip," the script girl, and the student assistant who learns by watching become caught up in the vision of what the screen can show: something more than an ephemeral experience. Producers and front-office men concerned with the distribution hope the product of artistic creation will be a good seller. Later, critics and audiences will determine whether the parts cohere, whether continuity, tempo, structural rhythm, imagery, tone, and theme function organically as significant art.

APPENDIX

Limitations in Film as a
Recorder of Reality

WHEN the architects of ancient Greece planned the construction of the Parthenon, they realized that in order to give the structure its desired symmetry and balance, they would have to cope with a curious defect in human perception. Whenever two horizontal lines are intersected by a series of perpendicular vertical ones, they appear, even though perfectly parallel, to curve in the middle. Thus if both the base line and the capital line which the upright columns are perpendicular to had been allowed to remain strictly parallel, the temple would have appeared to sag in the center. To compensate for the eye's refusal to see "reality" properly, the architects had to slightly curve both the base line and the capital line to give the illusion of parallelism. Whenever art tries to capture life or reality, it confronts, and must overcome, certain limitations inherent either in the human senses or in its own medium of expression. Because of convention or necessity, the sculptor forgoes movement and color, and the painter forgoes true scale and three-dimensionality.

Film also has its limitations, both inherent and conventional. Although the camera is patterned after that most complex recording device—the human eye—it neither "sees" nor "understands" precisely the same way the unencumbered eye does, for it is without the directive, controlling force that simultaneously selects and interprets reality—the mind. The attempt in *Lady in the Lake* to make the camera serve as the eyes of the protagonist would have failed even if the equipment had been as mobile as the lighter equipment of today and if all the physiological functions of the eye had been simulated. The subjective quality of the mind does not allow us to "see" the continual instants of blackness as the lids blink, nor are we aware of, much less traumatized by, the jarring movement of our bodies as we walk, or the jerky movement of the head as it turns. However, when faithfully simulated by a camera (today usually a hand-held camera) such effects are dizzying and irritating.

Like any other art, the art of the film accomplishes its most realistic effects through a series of conventions or oblique approaches to reality.* In film making the most obvious attempts to transcribe reality literally have been Technicolor, 3-D, and wide-screen—all of which have had a rather dubious success as "realism." They retain their gimmicky nature of ex-aggerated spectacle rather than inspire an engrossment in photographed reality. However in *Old and New*, Eisenstein's silent classic of 1929, the most photographically real events seem to be those which have their temporal and spatial relationships restructured by the film maker's editing. His oblique method of "analyzing" through a series of rapid shots the working parts of the peasants' new cream separator gives a more vivid impression of its dynamic nature (since the cutting itself is dynamic) than his more direct attempt at rendering movement when he straps a camera onto the end of a scythe blade cutting through a field of waving grass. Unfortunately in the latter instance the apparent fixity of the scythe in the center of the frame makes the background seem to move, and we feel that a landscape of grass is obligingly moving up against a stationary blade.

A more common phenomenon in which the realism of motion is de-feated by relativity when a direct attempt is made to record it is bound up with the mechanical function of the camera itself. We have all noticed how in westerns the wheels of a fast-moving stagecoach may seem for a moment to be revolving backward. This occurs whenever the speed at which the wheels are spinning exceeds the rate at which the film is passing through the camera during the filming. A sequence of frames following (Fig. 37) shows how the relative speeds affect and distort the recorded image. The cinematographer can remedy this defect by either slowing down the motion of the wagon or by increasing the rate at which the camera records.

There are many other ways in which "photographic reality" in the cinema is threatened by the limitations of the medium. But, as in the other arts, these very limitations challenge the artist to create conventions and tech-niques to transcend and heighten reality. The sacrifice of three-dimensionality

* As Max Beerbohm phrased it, "Life, save only through conventions, is inimitable. The more closely it be aped, the more futile and unreal its copy. . . . Good painting and good sculpture inspire us with some illusion, thus compensating us for what were otherwise the fatigue of gazing at them." ("Madame Tussaud's," *Works and More,* London: John Lane, 1952, pp. 152-53.) Elsewhere Beerbohm wrote: "For its power to illude, an art depends on its limitations. Art never can be life, but it may seem to be so if it do but keep far enough away from life. . . . If a painter swelled his canvas out and in according to the convexities and concavities of his model, or if a sculptor overlaid his material with authentic flesh-tints, then you would demand that the painted or sculptured figure should blink, or stroke its chin, or kick its foot in the air. That it could do none of these things would rob it of all power to illude you. An art that challenges life at close quarters is defeated through the simple fact that it is not life." (From "The Ragged Regiment," *Yet Again,* London: William Heinemann, Ltd., 1951, pp. 248-49.)

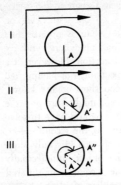

The wagon is moving to the right: therefore spoke A ought to appear to be moving clockwise. However in between the shooting of frame I and frame II the spoke had revolved to the A′ position. And by the time frame III was shot the spoke had reached A″. When projected in sequence, the frames reveal a counterclockwise, rather than clockwise, movement of the spoke.

Fig. 37. Distortion of recorded images through relative speed of image and frame.

in cinematography inspired Josef von Sternberg to create a compensating richness in texture and composition in his films. This he was able to achieve by such devices as shooting scenes through blinds and latticework (*Shanghai Express*, 1932, *Morocco*, 1930, and *Blond Venus*, 1932), through netting (the love scene in *The Scarlet Empress*) or through the spokes of a wagon wheel (the tavern scenes in *Docks of New York*, 1928). Different compositional planes were suggested by both the lines and the shadows cast by them, perhaps upon the floor or upon a back wall.

Motion itself, whether of object, camera, or background, adds dimensionality to a scene—the loss of which is very noticeable when a director chooses to freeze a scene in tableau. Movement of the camera toward an object, especially at an unusual angle, gives a greater three-dimensional illusion than movement laterally across it, for in the former instance objects in the foreground will seem to be moving into the camera faster than those in the background. (This effect, as we have noted, is not achieved with a zoom lens movement, in which all points, both in foreground and background, move at the same rate of speed.) An even better illusion of three-dimensionality, however, occurs when we are allowed to see an object revolve around its vertical axis because all parts and facets of the object will therefore move both laterally across the screen and in and out of depth. An opening door would be the most common occurrence of such a movement in three-dimensional illusion, but more dramatic examples would be the perpetually turning revolving door in Murnau's *The Last Laugh* (1924) and the low-angle shots of the cornices of large buildings in *Umberto D* (1952) as the streetcar carrying the old man swings around them.

Even though both the eye and the camera record happenings in fragments, singling out objects from an amorphous conglomeration, widening and narrowing the angle of vision of them, an observer who directs his own eyes is better able to maintain his orientation than one who has his eyes directed for him by the director of photography.* If we look at a chair in our living room, close our eyes, turn our head slightly, and then open our eyes on another very similar chair, we know that the second chair is not the first one because our mind and will prompted us to look elsewhere, and we remember the sensation of our head moving in that direction. However, if a film director cuts from one chair to the other, the spectator, not having had any sensation of the change in camera setups between shots or any knowledge that there was more than one chair in the room, might interpret the second chair as a second take of the first.† The director would have to solve this problem visually by panning to, rather than cutting to, the second object, thus maintaining the spatial relationships of the two objects. His only alternative would be to establish the relationship of the objects *intellectually* through the context of story line. If the shape of the second chair differed slightly from that of the first, there might still be a problem of identification, for in this instance the cut would make it appear as if the first chair had been *transformed* into the second. The remedy would perhaps again lie in substituting panning for cutting.

This problem occurs more usually under conditions in which panning cannot be used to reorient the viewer spatially. Take, for example, a sequence in which one fighter plane is pursuing another. If the airplanes are very similar in appearance, a cut to the second might seem to be a retake of the first, and panning from one to the other might be technically impossible because of their distance from each other. Furthermore, the problem probably could not be resolved by showing a fixed point in the sky which each plane could successively pass. Similarly the shot of a boat pursuing another of the same appearance might seem to be a second take of the first if there is no stationary point in the homogeneous background to mark their relative progress. The remedy in this instance might be to use a camera angle as the equivalent of a fixed point. In the following diagram, shot I shows object A approaching the center of the frame from right to left at an acute angle; shot II shows the object retreating to the left at an oblique angle away from the center of the frame. Shots III and IV of the pursuing object (B) are done by using the same change in angle—which itself functions as a fixed point

---

* Even so, some avant-garde film makers have tried to go a step further by having the medium simulate the way in which the eye "sees itself." We find Stan Brakhage talking about achieving on film the effects of an afterimage (when the eye closing on some bright image retains it for a moment), or the sensation of seeing specks floating before the eyes in bright daylight (caused by the sight of molecules of blood passing through the eye). The first of these he suggests by the subtle use of fades and dissolves or a shift from positive to negative image; the second effect he feels is rendered by the graininess of 8 mm film being projected on a large screen. (Introduction to a showing of his *Portraits* and *Songs* at the Filmmakers' Cinematheque in New York in the winter of 1965-66.)

† For the following observations concerning "second-take" effects and the problems of crossing the "stage line," the authors are indebted to Slavko Vorkapich, who introduced and developed these points in his lectures at the Museum of Modern Art in New York in the spring of 1965.

in that it suggests a definite coordinate point from which the camera is observing.

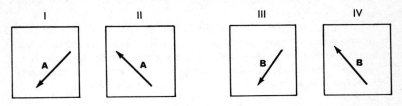

Fig. 38. Camera angles for spatial orientation.

Another problem in spatial orientation for the moviegoer may arise when the camera crosses the "stage line" in filming successive parts of a scene. If a member of a theater audience went backstage into the wings to witness the performance, he would not be surprised to see the "reverse side," as it were, of the stage action. Nor are moviegoers especially disconcerted by the many reverse-angle shots shown on the screen, usually occurring when two characters are confronting each other. However, when lateral movement of an object is occurring, the director's decision to cross the stage line for a reverse-angle shot might cause confusion because the directional line of movement reverses itself. The following illustration of a reverse-angle shot of a car actually traveling from right to left shows how this happens:

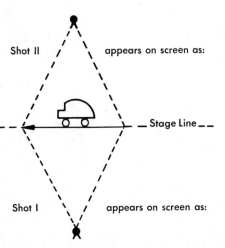

but the actual direction in which the car is moving is the same for both shots.

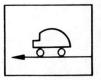

Fig. 39. Recognition of "stage line" in reverse-angle shots.

Unless the director somehow makes us aware that he is bringing the camera (and us along with it) across the stage line—possibly by interposing an immediate shot taken at the stage line itself—our photographic view of reality may become confused.

As a simple recorder of objective reality the motion picture camera is thus bedeviled by many hazards and ambiguities which clearly demonstrate that it does not see precisely the way the eye sees since it lacks the compensating illumination that the brain supplies to the eye or the unconscious physiological adjustments made by the body. Objective or photographic reality has a way of eluding the simple and direct gaze of a camera lens and can be approached only through a carefully calculated series of oblique maneuvers.

References

CHAPTER ONE
The Film Experience

1. Arthur Knight, *The Liveliest Art* (New York: The New American Library, 1957), pp. 152-53.
2. James Agee, *Agee on Film: Reviews and Comments* (Boston: Beacon Press, 1964), p. 112.
3. James Card, "George Eastman House Photography" in "Our Resources for Scholarship," *Film Quarterly*, XVI (Winter, 1962-63), p. 40.
4. Andrew Sarris, "The American Director's Issue," *Film Culture*, No. 28, (Spring, 1963), p. 58.

CHAPTER TWO
Continuity

1. Hortense Powdermaker, *Hollywood: The Dream Factory* (Boston: Little, Brown and Company, 1950), p. 14.
2. Erwin Panofsky, "Style and Medium in the Moving Picture," *Transition, a Quarterly Review*, Winter, 1937, pp. 121-33.
3. E. M. Forster, *Aspects of the Novel* (New York: Harcourt, Brace, 1927), p. 86. Quotation slightly altered.
4. Francis Fergusson, *The Idea of a Theatre* (Garden City, N.Y.: Doubleday, 1949), pp. 229-234.

CHAPTER THREE
Visual Rhythm Within the Shot

1. James Joyce, *The Portable James Joyce* (New York: Viking Press, 1947), pp. 481-82.
2. Robert Gessner, "The Seven Faces of Time," *Theater Arts*, XLVI (July, 1962), pp. 13-17.
3. Cleanth Brooks and Robert Penn Warren, *Understanding Poetry*, third edition (New York: Holt, Rinehart and Winston, 1961), p. 124.
4. Gessner, *loc. cit.*
5. Irving Howe, "Dreiser and the Tragedy," *New Republic*, August 22, 1964.
6. Andrew Sarris in the *Village Voice*, July 9, 1964.

7. Gessner, *loc. cit.*
8. "Shot," *Webster's Collegiate Dictionary*, third edition.
9. Raymond Spottiswoode, *A Grammar of the Film* (Berkeley: University of California Press, 1962), p. 44.
10. Gessner, *loc. cit.*
11. A. R. Fulton, *Motion Pictures: The Development of an Art* (Norman, Okla.: University of Oklahoma Press, 1960), p. 261.
12. Slavko Vorkapich, lectures on "The Visual Nature of Film" at the Museum of Modern Art, 1965.
13. Fulton, *op. cit.*, p. 237.

CHAPTER FOUR
Structural Rhythm

1. Fulton, *op. cit.*, p. 310.
2. Pare Lorentz, *The River: A Scenario* (New York: Stackpole & Sons, 1938).
3. Slavko Vorkapich, lectures on "The Visual Nature of Film" at the Museum of Modern Art, 1965.
4. Stan Brakhage, "Metaphors on Vision," *Film Culture* (Fall, 1963), section heading "State Meant: Notes on the Movement of the Animal Form at Night." There is no pagination in this issue.
5. Ivor Montague, *Film World* (Baltimore: Penguin Books, 1964), p. 126.
6. John Grierson, quoted in "Weinberg Scrap Books on Film, 1928," Museum of Modern Art Film Library, New York.
7. *Ibid.*
8. Penelope Houston, *The Contemporary Cinema* (Baltimore: Penguin Books, 1963), p. 91.
9. Roger Shattuck, *The Banquet Years* (New York: Harcourt, Brace, 1958), p. 134. See Satie's score reproduced.
10. Gessner, *loc. cit.*

CHAPTER FIVE
Imagery

1. Ezra Goodman, *The Fifty-Year Decline and Fall of Hollywood* (New York: Simon & Schuster, 1961), p. 292.
2. Jean Georges Auriol, *et al.*, *Le Cinema* (Paris: Aux Éditions du Cynge, 1932), p. 89.
3. Parker Tyler, *Chaplin: Last of the Clowns* (New York: Vanguard, 1947), p. 50.
4. Sergei Eisenstein, *The Film Sense* (New York: Meridian Books, 1957), pp. 256 ff.
5. Spottiswoode, *op. cit.*, p. 253.
6. Michelangelo Antonioni, *Screenplays* (New York: Orion Press, 1963), p. 211.
7. Federico Fellini, *La Dolce Vita*, trans. by Oscar De Liso and Bernard Shircliff (New York: Ballantine Books, 1961), p. 1.

8. *Ibid.*, p. 79.
9. *Ibid.*, p. 274.
10. Siegfried Kracauer, *From Caligari to Hitler* (New York: Noonday Press, 1947), p. 113.
11. Lewis Jacobs, *The Rise of the American Film* (New York: Harcourt, Brace, 1939), p. 199.
12. Carl Dreyer, "Thought on My Craft," *Sight and Sound,* XXV (Winter, 1955-56), pp. 128-29.
13. *Ibid.*, p. 129.
14. Parker Tyler, "The Horse: Totem Animal of the American Films," *Sight and Sound,* XVI (Autumn, 1947), pp. 112-14.
15. Lo Duca, *L'Erotisme au Cinema* (Paris: Jean-Jacques Pauvert, 1957), *passim.*

CHAPTER SIX
Tone and Point of View

1. Seymour Stern, "The Birth of a Nation: Part I," Special Griffith Issue, *Film Culture,* No. 36 (Spring-Summer, 1965), p. 86.
2. "Yasujito Ozu," *Film,* No. 36 (Summer, 1963), p. 9.
3. John Osborne, *Tom Jones: a Filmscript* (New York: Grove Press, 1964), p. 57.
4. Jonas Mekas, "Cinema of the New Generation," *Film Culture,* No. 21 (Summer, 1960), p. 15.
5. "Camera Three," CBS television program, Sunday, September 19, 1964.
6. Andrew Sarris in the *Village Voice,* November 12, 1964.
7. Evelyn Gerstein, *Theatre Arts Monthly,* XI (April, 1927), pp. 296-97.
8. Arthur Knight, *The Liveliest Art* (New York: New American Library, 1957), p. 303.
9. *Ibid.*, p. 304.

CHAPTER SEVEN
Theme

1. Seymour Stern, "The Birth of a Nation: Part I," Special Griffith Issue, *Film Culture,* No. 36 (Spring, 1965).
2. Gilbert Schloss, "The Great Comedians," *Film Notes of the Wisconsin Film Society,* edited by Arthur Lennig, Madison, Wisc., 1960, p. 81.
3. Herman G. Weinberg, "American Film Directors and Social Reality," *Sight and Sound,* VII (Winter, 1938-39), pp. 168-69.
4. *Ibid.*
5. *Ibid.*
6. Joseph L. Anderson and Donald Richie, *The Japanese Film* (New York: Grove Press, 1959), p. 380. See also Donald Richie, *Japanese Movies* (Tokyo: Japan Travel Bureau, 1961), pp. 153-54.
7. Bosley Crowther in the *New York Times,* February 9, 1965.

CHAPTER EIGHT
The Film Art

1. Andrew Sarris in the *Village Voice*, March 23, 1967.

Index